ATSUKO'S
JAPANESE
KITCHEN

ATSUKO'S
JAPANESE
KITCHEN

HOME-COOKED COMFORT FOOD MADE SIMPLE

ATSUKO IKEDA
Photography by YUKI SUGIURA

RYLAND PETERS & SMALL
LONDON • NEW YORK

Senior Designer Megan Smith
Design Assistance Emily Breen
Commissioning Editor
  Alice Sambrook
Art Director Leslie Harrington
Editorial Director Julia Charles
Production Controller
  Mai-Ling Collyer
Publisher Cindy Richards
Food Stylist Atsuko Ikeda
Prop Stylist Alexander Breeze
Indexer Hilary Bird
Illustrator Risa Sano/Mentsen

Published in 2019 by
Ryland Peters & Small
20–21 Jockey's Fields
London WC1R 4BW
and
341 East 116th Street
New York, NY 10029

www.rylandpeters.com

10 9 8 7 6 5 4 3 2

Text © Atsuko Ikeda 2019

Design, illustration and
commissioned photography
© Ryland Peters & Small 2019

ISBN 978-1-78879-081-9

A CIP record for this book is
available from the Brisih Library.
US Library of Congress CIP data
has been applied for.

Printed in China

NOTES
• Both British (Metric) and American
(Imperial plus US cups) measurements
are included in these recipes for your
convenience. However it is important
to work with one set of measurements
and not alternate between the two
within a recipe.

• All spoon measurements are
level unless otherwise specified.
• Uncooked or partially cooked eggs
should not be served to the very
old, frail, young children, pregnant
women or those with compromised
immune systems.
• When following a recipe which
uses raw fish, always ensure you buy
sashimi-quality ingredients and use
on the day of purchase. Raw fish
or meat should not be served to
the very old, frail, young children,
pregnant women or those with
compromised immune systems,
without medical advice.
• Ovens should be preheated
to the specified temperatures.
We recommend using an oven
thermometer. If using a fan-assisted
oven, adjust temperatures according
to the manufacturer's instructions.
• When a recipe calls for the grated
zest of citrus fruit, buy unwaxed fruit
and wash well before using. If you
can only find treated fruit, scrub well
in warm soapy water before using.

CONTENTS

MY JAPANESE KITCHEN

Japanese food is now one of the most popular cuisines in the world. In 2006, there were 24,000 Japanese restaurants around the globe, and by 2016, it had nearly quadrupled to 89,000! However, it is a cuisine still widely misunderstood. For most, it revolves around sushi, ramen, curry or miso soup... but it is so much more than that! Japan has an incredible variety of cuisines depending on its regions, but also such an interesting food culture. With subtle influence from foreign dishes over the centuries, it has adopted and refined them to make them its own. As you read through the recipes in this book, you'll hopefully enjoy recognizing some of the global influences!

I have been running my cooking classes in London for over 10 years now. I started doing so after feeling slightly homesick, living so far away from Japan. I really missed the food I grew up with, its flavours, the way we eat and the ceremony of it. So I decided to change this feeling of emptiness into something positive. Starting my cooking classes made me feel more connected to my roots and actually allowed me to understand them even better. Helping my students to grasp the essence of Japanese cuisine and become confident using Japanese products has been a two-way relationship. Thanks to my students, I now understand exactly what can be intimidating about Japanese cuisine, and the major points of difference between this and Western cooking. With this in mind, I have developed an approach to teaching that makes even novice cooks feel at ease after a bit of practice. This is what I want to share with you in this book.

I was told by some students that they had tried understanding Japanese food by studying books, but it's really only after completing my beginners' course that they 'got it', and felt confident cooking Japanese food at home. I wanted this book to work in a similar way. The goal is for you to understand the concept behind Japanese food, and to learn about dishes that have been cooked regularly in Japanese households for decades and sometimes centuries. I will give you inside tips and help you to make these dishes methodically, until eventually you won't need any recipes or measurements to create your own Japanese meals! It's about you acquiring essential knowledge and a few skills, in a fun and interesting way. Before you know it, you'll be able to cook a balanced and delicious Japanese meal, without feeling like you're about to climb Mount Fuji!

Atsuko's Japanese Kitchen is a *condensé* of more than 10 years of my cooking classes. I have included all the tried and tested recipes loved by my students and clients. In the first pages, I introduce you to the basic principles of Japanese cuisine, essential ingredients and equipment for your kitchen and the Japanese way of planning a meal with its different components. The book is then separated in chapters corresponding to these components (mains, sides etc...), so that you can choose from them depending on your occasion. Some of these recipes are very traditional, handed down through generations of my family, and others I have added a modern twist to. Hopefully, together they form a cookbook that you and your family will always go back to.

REGIONAL DISHES

Japan is home to eight major regions and 47 prefectures, from the islands of Okinawa in the south west, to Hokkaido in the north east, each with their own traditions and specialties. Being so expansive, Japan has a wide range of climates and landforms. One way to comprehend this is to follow the blossoming of the famous cherry blossoms or 'sakura'. The milder the climate, the earlier the blossoms open. So blossom season sweeps up the country from south to north, starting in sub-tropical Okinawa in late January, and making its way up to Hokkaido in mid-to-late May. Such variety in climate creates a diversity of agriculture dependant on the region, and with this its own cuisine and regional specialties otherwise known as 'Kyodo ryori'.

The **KYUSHU REGION**, where I am from, is the third largest island of Japan, located in the south west. It's the top producer of premium grade Japanese kurobuta (black pork), which you can find in local dishes such as Buta No Kakuni (page 134) or Tonkotsu Ramen (page 84). It has an interesting history, being the only Japanese gateway for trade with Korea and China, but also Portugal and the Netherlands, from the 17th until the 19th century. Kyushu's cuisine has various multicultural influences, for example Portuguese references in the Tempura (page 88) or Chicken Nanban (page 125). Mizutaki Nabe (page 128) is the pride of the port city of Hakata. The region is also famous for 'shochu', a distilled beverage.

SHIKOKU is the smallest of the four main islands, but it is not short of culinary delicacies. The local sanuki udon noodles are characteristically thick and springy and can be eaten in various ways from cold with a dipping sauce, to hot in a broth. Shikoku and its warm climate also lends itself to the cultivation of yuzu, the fragrant citrus fruit found in Yuzu Ponzu Dressing (page 168) among many other recipes.

The western **KANSAI REGION** has long been famous for its cuisine, and most of the Japanese dishes known around the world come from there. The savoury pancakes Okonomiyaki (page 65) are a staple in Kansai cooking, alongside the Kushikatsu skewers (page 52). In Kyoto and Nara prefectures, with their abundance of Buddhist temples, you'll also find delicate vegetarian dishes using tofu like Yudofu (page 129). The refreshing Hiyashi Somen (page 74) also come from this region, as well as the sweet and sticky dessert Mitarashi Dango (page 180).

The **CHUGOKU REGION**, located on the western part of the main Honshu island, also has some unforgettable delicacies such as the infamous poisonous fugu blowfish. Fugu is an expensive gourmet dish in Japan, and only a select guild authorized by the government of the city is allowed to prepare the dish.

The **CHUBU REGION** is the alpine region of Japan, located in the centre of Honshu. Some of the best agricultural producers can be found there, from soybean farms and miso production (used in Miso Soups, pages 76–77 and Nasu Dengaku, page 41) in Aichi to Niigata's top Koshihikari rice brand and sake.

The **KANTO REGION** is home to Tokyo as well as six other prefectures, all with their own distinct, delicious foods. Kanagawa, for example, is famous for its Katsu Curry (page 103) which has a sweet flavour and stew-like texture, very different from Indian or East Asian curry. It's also important to note the culinary battle between the Kanto and Kansai regions, Kanto-style Chirashizushi (page 112) is made with raw fish, unlike in the Kansai region, for example and the Kanto-style Sukiyaki Hot Pot (page 133), tends to be stronger in flavour than the Kansai-style.

TOHOKU is Honshu's remote and lush northern region, home to a multitude of delicacies such as the buckwheat soba noodles (page 92), with their toasted nutty flavours and many nabe hot pot dishes.

The country's northernmost prefecture, **HOKKAIDO** offers a wide variety of vegetables, seafood and surprisingly for Japan... dairy products! During autumn in Sapporo, the wild salmon return from the ocean to the Toyohira river. This prized salmon is found in many dishes such as the Chan Chan Yaki (page 142). Finally, some of the best kombu seaweed, the base of Dashi (page 23), is mainly harvested in different locations in Hokkaido.

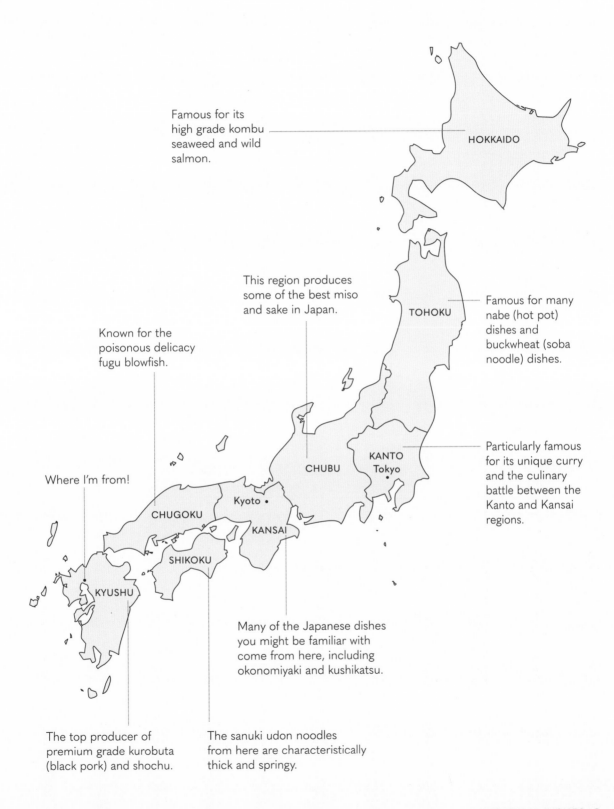

Famous for its high grade kombu seaweed and wild salmon.

HOKKAIDO

This region produces some of the best miso and sake in Japan.

TOHOKU

Famous for many nabe (hot pot) dishes and buckwheat (soba noodle) dishes.

Known for the poisonous delicacy fugu blowfish.

CHUBU

KANTO
Tokyo

Particularly famous for its unique curry and the culinary battle between the Kanto and Kansai regions.

Where I'm from!

CHUGOKU

Kyoto

KANSAI

SHIKOKU

KYUSHU

Many of the Japanese dishes you might be familiar with come from here, including okonomiyaki and kushikatsu.

The top producer of premium grade kurobuta (black pork) and shochu.

The sanuki udon noodles from here are characteristically thick and springy.

THE SECRETS OF JAPANESE CUISINE

THE GOLDEN RULE OF FIVE

When it comes to cooking a meal at home, how do you decide on what to make? Do you focus on seasonality or do you just use what's left in your fridge? Do you listen to what your body needs or do you give in to cravings? Sometimes the menu will depend on whether you are cooking for friends or family.

I'll let you into a little secret: whether you are cooking for one or 10 people, the most important thing to bear in mind is the perfect balance of the meal. This has been at the core of the philosophy of Japanese cuisine for centuries. In Japan, we've been following the magic 'rule of 5', which has been passed on through generations. This rule has created a population of healthy people with good appetites! The golden rule of five is very easy to follow, and even easier to remember: the perfectly balanced meal should have 五味 (gomi) – five tastes, 五色 (goshoku) – five colours and 五法 (gohou) – be prepared with five different cooking methods. This practical method of planning a meal truly helps you to have a balanced diet in your everyday life.

One final tip for you, be mindful of how much you eat. We have a saying in Japan that goes 'hara hachi bu', which means 'eat until your stomach is 80% full'. It will give you enough sustainable energy until your next meal, but your mind will remain sharp and clear without the feeling of tiredness you get from being overly full.

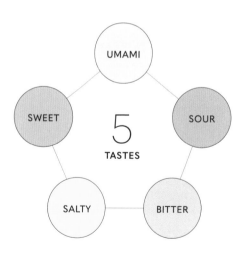

FIVE TASTES

The theory is, that if these tastes are all present in a meal, you won't have cravings because all the satisfactory flavours are already here. Japanese cuisine relies on six essential seasonings, representing the five tastes: soy sauce, miso, mirin, sake, rice vinegar and umami-rich dashi (see page 16). They are used to season most Japanese dishes. Spices can be added as a condiment to give extra vibrancy, but this is not considered necessary in Japanese cuisine. To put this into practice, choose a main dish with a dominant taste, then think of side dishes that offer the other missing tastes. This will balance the flavours in your main dish.

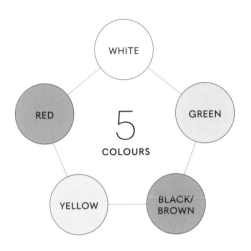

FIVE COLOURS

The idea behind this is to include a range of five ingredients in different colours in your meal. There are two main reasons for this: firstly, eating a rainbow of foods will provide you with a wide range of essential nutrients and minerals needed throughout your day. If you eat a moderate amount of every food group, you can be sure you are getting the nutrients you need! Secondly, on an aesthetic level, you eat with your eyes first. Food should be enjoyed with all your senses, and sight is very important in Japanese cuisine. The visual enjoyment of your meal will make it more appetizing!

FIVE COOKING METHODS

Think of an egg – there are many ways to cook it, and the eating experience can be so different considering you are starting with just the one same ingredient. Using a variation of these five cooking methods in a meal creates pleasing contrasts in texture. Fresh raw vegetables will be crunchy, while fried tempura will be crispy, boiled ingredients will be tender, etc. Mixing and matching these cooking methods will ensure the meals you serve will never be bland.

HOW TO PLAN
YOUR MEAL

A full traditional Japanese meal usually consists of five components: rice, a soup, a main and one or more side dishes, including some pickled vegetables. In every day cooking, this can be pared back to a main with some rice and soup and you can, of course, only have one dish if you don't feel that hungry or if you want to make something quick. If so, go for a 'One-plate meal' (pages 94–115). If you decide to eat the proper Japanese way with its five components, let me guide you on how to build your menu. First, decide on your main. Then, choose the other dishes to balance out your main. For example, if your main is a miso or soy-based dish, choose something sour like pickles as a side, or something refreshing like a leafy salad mixed with seaweed to balance out the saltiness of your main. The idea is to have your five tastes and five colours (see pages 10–11) represented in your menu. So after choosing your main, work by elimination to find the missing tastes and colours to pick your other dishes.

EATING IN A TRIANGLE WAY

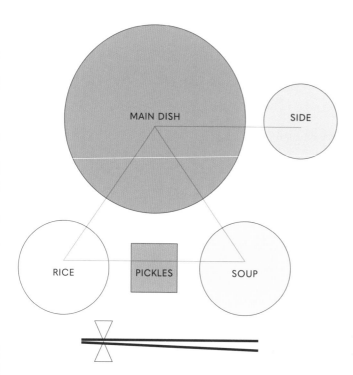

In Western cuisine, you might have three courses: appetizer, main and dessert, which are eaten one by one.

The basic formula for a traditional Japanese meal is rice, soup, a main and some side dishes, including pickled vegetables. Unlike in western countries, we serve our dishes together on one tray and eat them in a triangle way. By this, I mean, first, sip a little soup to wet your mouth, then eat some rice with some of the dishes on the tray like some sweet and salty teriyaki. All the various flavours and textures then harmonize in your mouth. You might cleanse your palate with the refreshing acidity of the pickles and then start again with the miso soup... and don't forget to say 'itadakimasu' before you eat!

SAMPLE MEAL PLANNER

	SAMPLE MEAL 1	SAMPLE MEAL 2	SAMPLE MEAL 3
MAIN	Chicken Teriyaki with Lime *p.111*	Fish Pillows & Clams with Yuzu Ponzu *p.141*	Fried Ginger Pork *p.107*
RICE	Rice & Quinoa *p.30*	Plain White Rice *p.29*	Plain White Rice *p.29*
SOUP	Miso Soup with Wakame & Tofu *p.76*	Miso soup with Watercress & Fried Tofu *p.76*	Fluffy Egg & Tomato Soup *p.107*
SIDE	Sesame Dressing on Green Beans *p.164*	Kimpira Salad *p.154*	Wakame & Cucumber Salad with Sesame Dressing *p.155*
PICKLES	Quick-pickled Vegetables *p.160*	Ume-flavoured Pickled Radishes *p.160*	Ume-flavoured Pickled *Radishes p.160*

SAMPLE COOKING TIMELINE

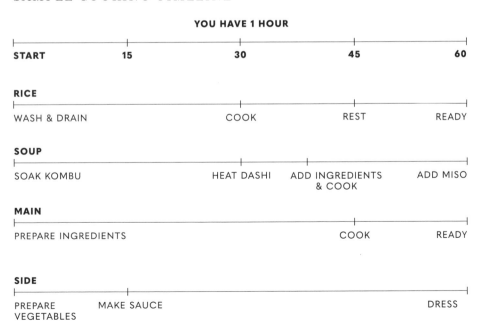

YOU HAVE 1 HOUR

START   15   30   45   60

RICE

WASH & DRAIN   COOK   REST   READY

SOUP

SOAK KOMBU   HEAT DASHI   ADD INGREDIENTS & COOK   ADD MISO

MAIN

PREPARE INGREDIENTS   COOK   READY

SIDE

PREPARE VEGETABLES   MAKE SAUCE   DRESS

5 JAPANESE CHOPSTICK MANNERS YOU SHOULD KNOW

Manners are of great cultural importance to Japanese people, and chopstick manners in particular are something you can easily learn and practice. If you are lucky enough to visit Japan, having a little knowledge about local manners is very important to show your respect, and it will deepen your experience as a tourist. Or, even if you are just eating in a Japanese restaurant or sharing a meal with Japanese friends, colleagues or clients, it is nice to show off your education of their culture. Some of the rules may not make sense to you, but each culture in the world has its own set of unique traditions for different reasons. Do bear in mind that chopstick manners may differ from culture to culture, and in China and Korea the chopstick rules are different. These are my top five easy Japanese rules to remember:

1. DO NOT TRANSFER FOOD FROM ONE PERSON'S CHOPSTICKS TO ANOTHER.
This is reserved for funerals, when the cremated bone is ritually transferred by two people with their chopsticks to an urn.

2. DO NOT HOLD CHOPSTICKS LIKE A KNIFE AND FORK.
I often see people in restaurants holding their chopsticks, one in each hand, and using them to saw through food as if they were a knife and fork. This is not elegant! If the piece of food is too large for you to eat in one go, simply use your chopsticks to break it by keeping the chopsticks together in one hand and sinking them down into the food to gently divide it into bite-sized pieces. It is also totally acceptable to ask a waiter to provide you with a knife and fork. However, skilled chefs should be aware of how their food is eaten, and should serve dishes that are not a battle to eat!

3. DO REVERSE YOUR CHOPSTICKS WHEN PICKING UP FOOD FROM COMMUNAL DISHES.
Take food from shared serving dishes using separate serving utensils or reverse your chopsticks and use the clean end, you can then wipe off the used end with a clean cloth or napkin. Place the food on your own bowl or serving plate before eating it.

4. DO NOT STICK YOUR CHOPSTICKS VERTICALLY INTO RICE OR FOOD.
This is an absolute NO at the table, as it is associated with death. This is the way one offers a bowl of rice to a dead person in front of their photograph at the Buddhist altar.

5. DO USE A CHOPSTICK REST PROPERLY.
When your chopsticks are not being used, put the pointed ends on a chopstick rest with them in front and parallel to you. If you are right-handed, put the tips on the left-hand side and if you are left-handed, put the tips on the right-hand side.

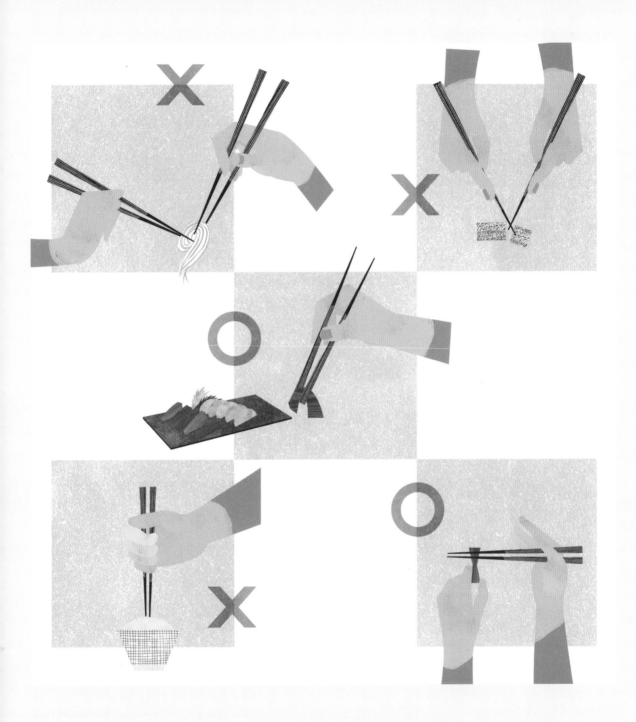

ESSENTIAL INGREDIENTS

There is huge variety in Japanese cuisine, and people often wonder how the complex umami flavours are achieved. In fact, you can make hundreds of Japanese dishes with little more than the five essential seasonings listed below: soy sauce, mirin, sake, rice vinegar and miso, which no Japanese pantry should be without. These ingredients encompass the five tastes that we crave (see page 10), so you will always feel satisfied after eating a meal. I have also listed below some other key Japanese ingredients used frequently throughout this book, that you may or may not be familiar with. Once you understand how to use these ingredients, you will have the tools you need to begin cooking!

5 ESSENTIAL SEASONINGS

1. SHOYU (SOY SAUCE)
Made of fermented soybeans, wheat and salt, shoyu or soy sauce is used in almost every Japanese meal. There are three main kinds of Japanese soy sauce: koikuchi (dark soy sauce) is by far the most common, and is therefore simply referred to as 'soy sauce' throughout this book. Usukuchi or light soy sauce has more salt added, so it tastes a bit saltier but less fermented than dark soy sauce. Its paler colour won't darken the colour of your natural ingredients so much. For a wheat-free option, choose tamari soy sauce, which is also the richest in texture and flavour.

2. MIRIN (SWEET RICE WINE)
Also called 'hon mirin' (real mirin), this is a sweet sake used for seasoning many dishes, such as teriyaki sauce and stews. It is made from steamed rice, rice koji (cultured rice) and alcohol, and its delicate natural sweetness develops during the fermentation process. It is good for using in glazes that require a sweet-sticky finish. Because of its wine-like alcohol content, mirin should be cooked off over a high heat to burn off the alcohol. If you prefer a non-alcoholic option, alcohol-free mirin is also available.

3. SAKE (RICE WINE)
Just like wine in the West, sake can be enjoyed both as an alcoholic drink (see page 31) and used as a cooking ingredient. It removes strong smells from fish, seafood and meat but also helps other flavours in the dish to penetrate. If you aren't sure which to use, specialist cooking sake is available (just like cooking wine), which is normally seasoned with salt.

4. SU (RICE VINEGAR)
Rice vinegar is the most common vinegar in Japan, but brown rice or grain vinegars are also available. Rice vinegar has a mild flavour, a low acidity and is pale yellow in colour. It is essential for ponzu, dipping sauce for gyoza and in sweet and sour dishes. It is also used as sushi vinegar.

5. MISO (FERMENTED SOYBEAN PASTE)
Miso is a deeply savoury, intense fermented paste made from soybeans and sea salt combined with koji culture (a mould starter). There are many different types of miso available (see page 26). It's an essential seasoning in soups, marinades, dressings and more.

OTHER SEASONINGS

6. NERI GOMA (SESAME PASTE)
Nutty and aromatic, both black and white sesame seeds are frequently used in Japanese cuisine. Japanese sesame paste is similar to tahini, but is normally made with unhulled sesame seeds (whereas tahini is usually made with hulled). The seeds also tend to be roasted for longer, giving a nuttier taste. This paste is used in many dressings and sauces.

7. SHIO KOJI (FERMENTED RICE KOJI & SALT)
This is a fermented seasoning made of rice koji, salt and water. It can be used to pickle vegetables or to marinade, enhance the flavour of and tenderize fish and meat. You can buy shio koji in liquid or paste form, but making it at home has become hugely popular in Japan as it is so simple to prepare.

8. UMEBOSHI (SALTED PICKLED PLUMS)

Umeboshi are tart and salty pickled plums, which had medicinal uses in ancient times, but have now become everyday food in Japan. Umeboshi products also include liquid seasonings or purées.

9. SHICHIMI (JAPANESE SPICE MIX)

A blend of seven ingredients, typically comprising of ground red chilli/chili pepper, sansho pepper, dried orange zest, sesame seeds, hemp seeds, green nori flakes and dried ginger. This can be sprinkled on noodle soups, grilled meat and rice bowl dishes.

10. YUZU KOSHO (YUZU & CITRUS CHILLI PASTE)

A paste made from yuzu zest, green chilli/chili and salt, this is usually served as a condiment.

11. YUZU JUICE

The yuzu has an aromatic, tangy flavour that is distinct from any other citrus fruit, somewhat akin to a cross between grapefruit and lime. It is famously used in the Yuzu Ponzu Dressing (see page 168).

SEAWEED & MUSHROOMS

12. WAKAME SEAWEED

Dark green in colour, soft and mild in flavour, you might recognize this seaweed as the one you'd find floating in miso soup. Usually available dried, it can be quickly reconstituted in 5 minutes in water, added directly into hot soup or mixed into salads.

13. HIJIKI SEAWEED

This seaweed resembles a tea leaf when dried and looks like a black twig when reconstituted. Soak it in plenty of water for around 15 minutes and allow it to swell up to eight times its size before using. It has a crunchy texture and is rich in minerals and calcium.

14. KOMBU (KELP)

This seaweed is packed full of strong umami flavour, therefore its most important use is in dashi stock (see page 23), which is a base for many other dishes.

15. HOSHI SHIITAKE (DRIED SHIITAKE MUSHROOMS)

These are really valuable for the flavour-punch they pack, and are used in another variation of dashi stock (see page 24). They need to be reconstituted before use, or can be used after making the dashi.

RICE & NOODLES

16. KOME (RICE)

The staple carbohydrate in Japanese cuisine! See more information on methods on page 29.

17. SOBA (BUCKWHEAT) NOODLES

Soba noodles made with a combination of buckwheat and wheat flours are widely available. For a guaranteed gluten-free option, some brands (available in specialist Japanese or health stores) use 100% buckwheat, which gives a lovely nutty taste. Soba noodles are usually either served chilled with a dipping sauce, or in hot broth as a noodle soup.

UDON NOODLES

Thick and chewy wheat flour noodles, these are the most satisfying and filling type of noodles. Delicious in all manner of stir-fries and soups.

18. SOMEN NOODLES

Somen noodles are a thinner version of udon (wheat) noodles. They make a light, refreshing meal and cook in just 2 minutes.

RAMEN NOODLES

These thin wheat noodles with pleasing elasticity were originally imported from China, but have gone on to feature in some of the most iconic and well-loved dishes in Japanese cuisine.

19. SHIRATAKI (WHITE WATERFALL) NOODLES

The translation 'white waterfall', refers to the appearance of these noodles. They are made from the konnyaku vegetable. As the end product consists of 97% of water, they are known as 'slim' noodles. Their gelatinous texture works in stews and hot pots.

TOFU & OTHER

20. TOFU (BEAN CURD)
This super-versatile ingredient comes in two main types: firm and silken. Both are made from soybeans, nigari (a coagulant) and at least 90% water. Depending on the recipe, water sometimes needs to be pressed out before you use the tofu.

21. ABURAAGE (THINLY-SLICED DEEP-FRIED TOFU)
Aburaage is ready-prepared deep-fried tofu slices. They are deep-fried in oil until fluffy and swelled, then deep-fried again at a higher temperature to crisp the outer skin. Like pitta breads, you can cut them in half to create a pocket which is used for stuffing. Aburaage is most famously used to make inari sushi and in miso soup and salads.

KONNYAKU BLOCK
Made from 97% water and konnyaku (root vegetable) powder, this Japanese health food adds texture to meat-free dishes. It's sold dried or in water, and can be white or brown (with added seaweed) in colour.

22. PANKO (JAPANESE BREADCRUMBS)
Panko are made from bread without crusts, which gives large, airy flakes that provide a light and crunchy coating. These are fantastic for chicken katsu, croquettes and even stuffings.

23. KATAKURIKO (POTATO STARCH)
A fine starch extracted from potatoes, this is becoming more available in free-from stores. It is used for coating ingredients before frying, thickening soups and sauces, or dusting wagashi. It can be substituted for cornflour/cornstarch if needed.

24. KATSUOBUSHI (BONITO FLAKES)
Katsuobushi, translated as 'bonito flakes', is a dried, fermented and smoked bonito (a type of tuna fish) which is shaved into flakes. This umami-rich ingredient is mostly used to make dashi stock (see page 24) or as a pretty topping for okonomiyaki.

USEFUL TOOLS

1. DONABE (EARTHENWARE COOKING POT)
A traditional Japanese earthenware pot, donabes are useful for cooking hot pots, stews, soups and rice. Because they are made from a special type of clay, these pots can withstand high temperatures and can be set over an open flame (though they can't be used with electric or induction hobs/stove-tops). Donabes build heat slowly, just like a slow cooker. Perfect for a family or group gathering, meals are often cooked in a donabe on the dining table over a portable gas stove. After the dish is cooked, we place the donabe on a round straw mat to avoid burning the table and serve the food straight from the pot.

2. OTOSHI BUTA (DROP-LID)
Useful for many of the stews in this book, a drop-lid sits directly on top of ingredients while they are simmering. It helps to prevent food from drying out as it cooks, and keeps fragile ingredients from breaking apart. It also distributes heat evenly to the dish as it is cooking and lets seasonings more easily penetrate. Drop-lids are usually made out of wood, and should be slightly smaller in diameter than the saucepan you are using.

If you haven't got one, you can make a disposable drop-lid using a sheet of greaseproof paper: take a big piece of greaseproof paper and cut it into a square. Fold the lower left corner over to its opposite corner to make a triangle. Rotate the triangle anti-clockwise to have the longer side facing you. Fold the left corner onto the right corner to make another smaller triangle. Now fold the right corner onto the upper corner and repeat once more. You should end up with a skinny triangle that looks almost like a paper plane (see page 21).

Now measure the radius of your pan by placing the tip of the triangle in the middle of the pan and trimming off the excess paper (following the rounded curve of the pan) that sticks out over the side. The paper should sit just inside the pan and not rest on the rim. Cut 3–4 slits on the folded sides for ventilation. Open the paper triangle out and place on top of the simmering dish.

3. SHAMOJI (RICE SPATULA)

This utensil, in the shape of a large, flat paddle with a rounded head, is used specifically for mixing and serving cooked rice. Traditionally made out of wood, it can now commonly be found made from plastic, too. Make sure you wet the spoon before handling your rice, so that the grains don't stick.

4. CONTAINER WITH DRYING RACK

This tray and rack set is designed for letting oil drain away after deep-frying foods. Used instead of draining oil on paper towels, this helps to keep long-lasting crispness in fried foods. The set can be substituted with a wire cooling rack or grill/broiler pan rack set over an oven tray.

5. SURIKOGI & SURIBACHI (PESTLE & MORTAR)

Suribachi literally means 'grinding-bowl' and surikogi translates to 'grind-powder-wood'. These are brilliant tools for grinding seeds, nuts or spices into a smooth paste. The difference between this and a Western pestle and mortar is the tiny grooves on the surface of the bowl, which really break down the ingredients. To use this properly, rub the stick one way against the bowl without bashing. Suribachi and sticks are sometimes sold separately, so make sure you get a suitable (larger in length) stick to go with your bowl. To clean, soak the bowl in hot water to loosen the ingredients that may be stuck between the grooves, then use a small brush to remove them.

6. SMALL DECORATIVE CUTTERS

Presentation is important in Japanese cuisine! Use these just like cookie cutters for making decorative garnishes out of vegetables like raw carrots, mushrooms or radishes, for celebrations or themed parties. The stainless steel cutters are available in a variety of shapes, such as stars and flowers. I keep mine in the wooden box (pictured), which is actually also used for measuring out rice.

7. OROSHIKI (JAPANESE GRATER)

You will love this tool once you get to know it! Unlike other graters, Japanese graters don't have perforated surfaces, so all the grated ingredient remains on the surface of the grater (rather than some collecting on the other side) and turns into a very fine paste. The metal version is used for drier ingredients, such as garlic, wasabi, etc, while the round ceramic one is useful for things like ginger, radishes etc, as you can collect the juice at its rim. Make sure to grate in a circular motion, rather than up and down.

8. SANTOKU HOCHO (ALL-PURPOSE KNIFE)

A santoku knife is versatile and can be used for three preparation techniques – chopping, slicing and mincing vegetables. Indeed, 'santoku' translates as 'three virtues'. You're not just limited to vegetables – santoku knives are more than up to the task of fish and meat preparation, too.

9. MISOKOSHI (MISO STRAINER)

If you're into your miso soup, this is a very useful tool! It helps the miso integrate into your dashi stock without forming any lumps, and it separates the grain from the paste if you are using a grainy miso. To use, put the miso in the strainer, attach the handle with the integrated hook to the inside of the saucepan so the miso is immersed in the dashi, and mix with a spoon to gently push the miso through. Discard the remaining grains in your strainer. Otherwise, a regular metal sieve/strainer will do a similar job.

10. AKUTORI (SKIMMER)

As the name of this tool suggests, the purpose of this tool is to 'skim the scum off'. This fine-mesh flat ladle is particularly useful for clearing the surface of stocks, soups and hot pots as they simmer. This keeps the soup clear and gives it a more refined taste, removing any debris or bitterness.

KOMBU DASHI

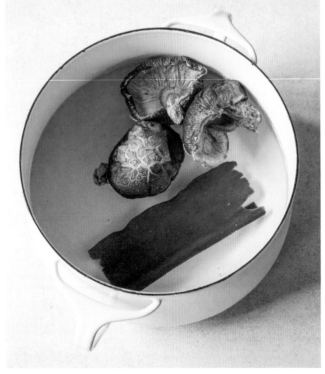

KOMBU & SHIITAKE DASHI

DASHI

Dashi literally translates as 'to extract'. Unlike other kinds of broth, Japanese broth is mainly based on dried ingredients such as kombu, katsuobushi (bonito flakes) and shiitake mushrooms, which have delicate yet intense characteristically umami-rich flavours (see below), that can be extracted in a relatively short time. Dashi is an ingredient at the heart of Japanese cuisine, and is used as the base of many traditional dishes. Thanks to the well-established ancient techniques of dashi-making, you will be surprised at how simple and quick it is to make proper dashi from scratch. Although, of course, like everything, instant powdered versions of dashi are available if you are very short on time.

WHAT IS UMAMI?

You may have heard of the term 'umami', also known as 'the fifth taste'. Scientifically identified by professor Kikunae Ikeda in 1908, it completes the other four tastes (sweet, sour, salty and bitter) and can be broadly understood as a very intensely savoury taste.

Far from an abstract concept, further research has shown that ingredients with amino acid glutamate and others containing either inosinic or guanylic acid are umami-potent.

Umami is found in a wide range of familiar ingredients and products such as tomatoes (especially sun-dried tomatoes and ketchup), anchovies, Parmesan cheese, cured meats, marmite/yeast extract and fish sauce. As a rule of thumb, anything fermented or cured contains umami.

Umami is valuable to cooks for many reasons: it draws out the flavours of other ingredients in a dish, adds a depth and satisfying savoury flavour, balances the overall taste of a dish and reduces the need for additional salt.

KOMBU DASHI

Kombu has been widely used in Japanese cuisine for over a thousand years, and you might call it the king of seaweed in terms of flavour potency. Kombu dashi is the favoured type of stock in shojin ryori (Buddhist vegan cuisine). There are different varieties of kombu, each with slightly different flavours – Rishiri, Hidaka, Rausu and Makombu are the most common. All of these are mainly harvested in Hokkaido in Northern Japan.

The surface of kombu is powdery-white, but don't mistake it for dust or mould. This is the sweet component called mannitol, which comes from the kombu during the drying process, and it should never be washed away. Nowadays, kombu is sold already clean. There are two ways of making kombu dashi. Simply soak the kombu in cold water overnight to draw out its elegant flavour, or soak it quickly in heated water for a richer, deeper flavour. The recipe below is for the latter method:

1 litre/quart cold water
10 g/¼ oz. (5 x 10-cm/2 x 4-inch) piece of kombu

MAKES 1 LITRE/QUART

Place the water and kombu in a large saucepan and let it soak for at least 30 minutes.

After 30 minutes, start to gently bring the water to the boil over a medium-high heat. Just before it reaches boiling point – when small bubbles appear at the bottom of the pan – remove the kombu and take the pan off the heat. The temperature should reach no more than about 60°C (140°F). Do not let the kombu boil; if you do the flavour will be spoilt. The kombu dashi is now ready to use. It will keep in the refrigerator in a sealed container for up to 3 days. You can use the same piece of kombu again to make another dashi, or dice and add it to soups or salads.

TIP The quality of water is as important for dashi as it is for brewing tea, so a soft or filtered water is ideal.

KOMBU & SHIITAKE DASHI

This stock is useful in any vegetarian dish. The dried shiitake mushrooms add an extra earthy depth of flavour to the broth. The magic, umami-rich combination of both kombu and shiitake, really enhances the flavour of any ingredient it pairs with. You can keep both the rehydrated shiitake mushrooms and kombu for use in other recipes.

1 litre/quart cold water
10 g/¼ oz. (5 x 10-cm/2 x 4-inch) piece of kombu
20 g/¾ oz. dried shiitake mushrooms

MAKES 800 ML/3⅓ CUPS

Place the water, kombu and shiitake mushrooms in a large saucepan and leave them to soak for at least 30 minutes.

After 30 minutes, start to gently bring the water to the boil over a medium-high heat. Just before it reaches boiling point – when small bubbles appear at the bottom of the pan – remove the kombu. Do not let the kombu boil; if you do the flavour will be spoilt. Continue heating to bring the water and mushrooms to the boil.

Once boiling, reduce the heat to low and simmer, uncovered, for 10 minutes. Skim any scum off the surface of the dashi as it cooks.

Turn the heat off and strain the dashi through a muslin/cheesecloth or paper towel-lined fine-mesh sieve/strainer. The dashi is now ready to use. It will keep in the refrigerator in a sealed container for up to 3 days.

TIP I wouldn't recommend freezing any dashi, it is easy to make and the flavours would not survive.

KOMBU & KATSUOBUSHI DASHI

This is the most common dashi (for non-vegetarians). It uses both kombu and katsuobushi (bonito flakes) together for an umami-rich dashi with a complex, deep flavour. When a recipe in this book refers to this dashi, you would usually make the ichiban dashi or 'primary dashi', which, with its refined, clean flavour, is perfect for clear soups, egg dishes or noodles in broth where the dashi is the primary flavour. Niban dashi or 'second dashi' uses the leftover ingredients from the ichiban dashi to make a second stock. This second dashi is less refined but still flavoursome – it is good for mixing into rich stews, glazes or pre-boiling vegetables to add flavour.

ICHIBAN DASHI (PRIMARY DASHI)
1 litre/quart cold water
10 g/¼ oz. (5 x 10-cm/2 x 4-inch) piece of kombu
20 g/¾ oz. katsuobushi (bonito flakes)

MAKES 800 ML/3⅓ CUPS

Place the water and kombu in a large saucepan and leave to soak for at least 30 minutes.

After 30 minutes, start to gently bring the water to the boil over a medium-high heat. Just before it reaches boiling point – when small bubbles appear at the bottom of the pan – remove the kombu and continue heating. Once boiling, turn the heat off and sprinkle the katsuobushi (bonito flakes) into the kombu dashi. Leave to brew for 2 minutes, letting the flakes sink to the bottom of the pan.

Strain the dashi through a muslin/cheesecloth or paper towel-lined fine-mesh sieve/strainer, letting it drip through. The finished dashi will keep in the refrigerator in a sealed container for up to 3 days.

NIBAN DASHI VARIATION (SECOND DASHI)
Place the reserved kombu and katsuobushi (bonito flakes) from the ichiban dashi in 1 litre/quart of fresh cold water in a saucepan. Start to bring to the boil. Just before it reaches boiling point, lower the heat and cook gently for 10 minutes. Strain the dashi through a muslin/cheesecloth or paper towel-lined fine-mesh sieve/strainer. Squeeze through the cloth.

KOMBU & KATSUOBUSHI DASHI

MISO

A staple seasoning in Japanese cuisine, miso is a fermented paste with a deep umami flavour. It is made from soybeans and sea salt combined with koji culture (a type of mould starter). The koji culture in miso can be made from any grains, such as brown or white rice, barley or soybeans, though 80% of miso in Japan is made with rice koji (rice culture).

There are many types of miso available to buy, but it is also very easy to make at home. I make my own miso every year by steaming and then mashing soybeans before mixing with rice koji (rice culture) to start the fermentation process. I then add salt according to the type of miso I want to make (the average salt content should be 10–12%). Once mixed, the fermentation starts and can take anywhere from three months to three years! The longer the fermentation process, the darker the miso and the more intense the flavour becomes.

Miso should be kept refrigerated to stop the fermentation process and preserve its freshness. You can also store it in the freezer – miso doesn't freeze so you can just use it straight away.

TYPES OF MISO

There are many different types of miso. These are broadly categorized into colours, from 'white' (pale yellow), to brown and red. The flavours range from sweet to salty and aromatic, while their textures can be smooth or grainy.

Miso is used in a variety of Japanese dishes, the most common of which are miso soups, marinades, sauces and dressings. You can also use miso outside of Japanese recipes, too, for interesting twists on classic recipes. I like to add it to butter or cream to give a richness, or to soups for depth of flavour.

How to choose the right miso depends on your preference, or the other flavours in your dish. Here, I have listed and described the most common types, which are suggested for use throughout this book. However, as long as you are aware of the qualities of the miso you have bought, you can mix and match a bit to your preference.

SAIKYO MISO (SWEET WHITE MISO)

This elegant, sweet and salty paste is the most popular type of miso in Kyoto, and is the miso of choice in the globally popular variations of the miso-marinated fish dish. It differs from other types of white miso in that it uses more rice koji, and the salt content is lower – typically around 5%. The natural sweetness comes from the additional rice koji and therefore the more intense fermentation.

SHIRO MISO (WHITE MISO)

This is a pale yellow, smooth paste made from soybeans and rice koji. The saltiness may vary in different brands, but it is generally mild and light in flavour. It's an extremely versatile miso, perfect in soups, marinades, dressings or even desserts.

AKA MISO (RED MISO)

Using the same ingredients as the shiro miso, aka miso gets its darker colour and deep aromatic flavour from its longer fermentation (over one year). Its texture can be smooth or grainy. Because of its stronger taste, it's perfect in sauces and stews.

GENMAI MISO (BROWN RICE MISO)

This is my favourite! Made from soy beans and brown rice, it has a medium-rich flavour, but with all the great nutritional benefits of brown rice. This can be used in the same dishes as aka miso.

OTHER TYPES OF MISO

MUGI MISO (BARLEY MISO)

Made from barley and soy beans, mugi miso is the most common type of miso in the Kyushu region. It is usually grainy and malty in taste.

HATCHO MISO (SOYBEAN MISO)

While other miso pastes are made with grains like rice and barley in the koji as well as soybeans, hatcho miso is made almost entirely from soybeans. Its dark brown colour and intense flavour (though surprisingly less salty) comes from a long ageing process.

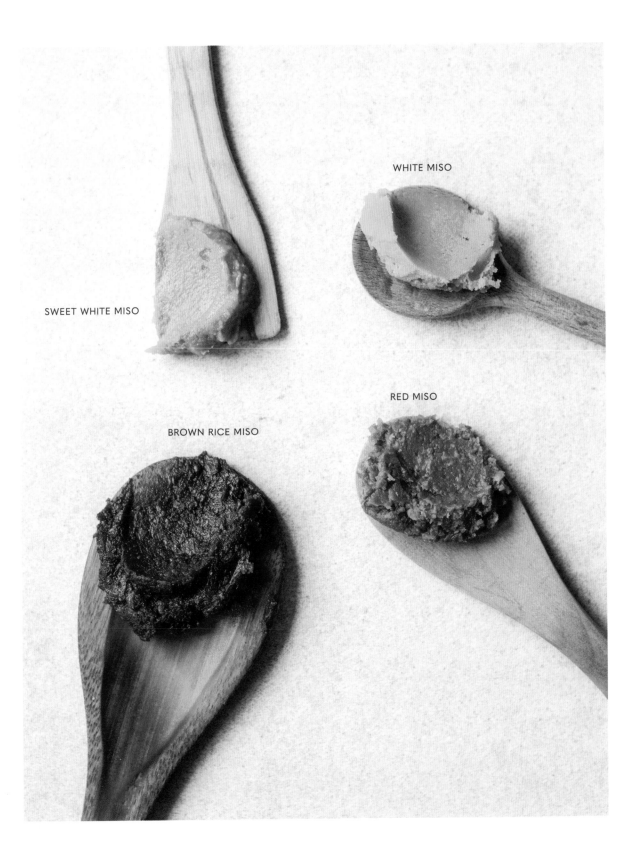

SWEET WHITE MISO

WHITE MISO

BROWN RICE MISO

RED MISO

RICE

The staple carbohydrate in Japanese cuisine, cooked rice is known as 'gohan', while uncooked rice is called 'kome'. The term 'gohan' also refers to a set meal, which consist of rice, soup and other dishes (see examples on page 12).

Japanese rice is unique because of its short, round grain and glutinous texture which, when cooked, makes it easy to pick up with chopsticks and mould into sushi. This type of rice is called Japonica rice and is grown all over the world in temperate climates, predominantly in Japan and Korea, though California, Italy and Spain are also big producers.

There are many sub-species of Japonica rice grown in Japan, but the most popular types are koshihikari, sasanishiki and akitakomachi. I would suggest using Japonica rice grown in Japan in one of these varieties for the best authentic results.

In grocery stores and supermarkets you will sometimes find japonica rice labelled 'sushi rice', as sushi is one of its most common uses, but it is actually just all-purpose Japanese rice, only when you add sushi vinegar does it become sushi rice!

Though white rice is the most traditional, modern Japanese cuisine recognises the health benefits of quinoa and brown rice, too, and they can be just as delicious! Here, are three different options for cooked rice, which you can combine with many of the dishes in this book.

SERVING GUIDE

You will need between 75–100 g/2½–3½ oz. uncooked rice per portion, but it depends on the type of meal you are serving. I would suggest making about 150 g/5½ oz. cooked rice per serving, if serving rice alongside a few other dishes. For a donburi (rice bowl) dish, you will need a bit more as rice is a main part of the dish, so about 200 g/7 oz. per serving.

PLAIN WHITE JAPANESE RICE

The most common and traditional option in Japan, this will go with any dish.

400 g/14 oz. Japanese short-grain rice
480 ml/2 cups water

MAKES 800 G/1¾ LB. (4–6 PORTIONS)

Place the rice in a sieve/strainer and wash under cold running water until the water becomes almost clear. Leave the rice to drain in the sieve/strainer for 30 minutes. This will allow the grains to slowly absorb the water that remains on the surface, which will help it to cook evenly.

Place the rice and water in a medium heavy-based saucepan and cover with a lid (don't remove the lid until the rice has rested). Bring to the boil over a high heat. It needs to be at a full boil, so wait until there is steam coming out from under the lid.

When the rice starts to boil, turn down to the lowest heat and simmer for the appropriate time, depending on the amount of rice. Refer to the table on page 31 for the correct amount of water and appropriate cooking time. The general rule or ratio to follow is 1:1.2 (or 20% more water than rice). I measure out my rice in a pyrex glass measuring jug/pitcher and then use the same vessel to measure the water, using 1 cup of rice to 1.2 cups of water. How simple is that!

When the cooking time is up, remove the pan from the heat, leave the lid on and rest for 10 minutes. All the water should be absorbed by the rice.

JAPANESE RICE & QUINOA

Quinoa adds protein and other nutritional benefits to your meal, but also an accent in firm texture while the stickiness of the white rice remains. You can also mix it up by using other kinds of healthy grains such as millet, amaranth, black or red rice, etc. Just replace 10% of the rice quantity with the grains. Note that you may need to soak some harder grains before cooking, depending on what you are using.

360 g/12⅔ oz. Japanese short-grain rice
40 g/1½ oz. mixed red and black quinoa
480 ml/2 cups water

MAKES 800 G/1¾ LB. (4–6 PORTIONS)

Place the rice and quinoa in a fine-mesh sieve/strainer and wash under cold running water until the water becomes almost clear. Leave the rice to drain in the sieve/strainer for 30 minutes. This will allow the grains to slowly absorb the water that remains on the surface, which will help it to cook evenly.

Place the rice, quinoa and water in a large heavy-based saucepan and then cover with a lid (don't remove the lid until the rice has rested). Bring to the boil over a high heat. When the rice starts to boil, turn down to the lowest heat and simmer for the appropriate time, depending on the amount of rice (see the chart, right).

When the cooking time is up, remove the pan from the heat, leave the lid on and rest for 10 minutes. All the water should be absorbed by the rice and quinoa.

JAPANESE BROWN RICE & PEARL BARLEY

The nutritional value of brown rice is well known. I choose brown rice with barley for the full nutritional value of the grains, higher fibre and texture. Try cooking it in a pressure cooker – it will guarantee a better, sticky texture and will reduce the cooking time by half.

PRESSURE COOKER METHOD
220 g/8 oz. Japanese brown rice
30 g/1 oz. pearl barley
400 ml/1/¾ cups water

MAKES 650 G/23 OZ. (4 PORTIONS)

Wash the brown rice and barley, then cover with fresh water and let soak in a bowl of water for at least 2 hours or overnight. Drain the rice.

Place the brown rice and barley in a pressure cooker with the water. Put the lid on and bring to the boil over a high heat. When the rice has reached high pressure, reduce to the lowest heat and simmer for 15 minutes.

Remove the saucepan from the heat and leave the lid on for 10 minutes for the pressure to slowly release.

SAUCEPAN METHOD
220 g/8 oz. short-grain brown rice
30 g/1 oz. pearl barley
500 ml/2 cups plus 2 tbsp water

MAKES 650 G/23 OZ. (4 PORTIONS)

Follow the same process as above but simmer for 30 minutes after boiling the rice.

WHITE JAPANESE RICE – QUICK REFERENCE CHART

Cooked rice	400 g/14 oz.	800 g/1¾ lb.	1.2 kg/2⅔ lb.
Uncooked rice	200 g/7 oz.	400 g/14 oz.	600 g/21 oz.
Water	240 ml/1 cup	480 ml/2 cups	720 ml/3 cups
Simmering time (after boiling)	9 minutes	12 minutes	15 minutes
Resting time	10 minutes	10 minutes	10 minutes

LEFTOVER RICE

If you have leftover cooked rice, do not throw it away. It will keep well in the fridge overnight for use in other dishes the next day (though do not eat leftover refrigerated rice that is more than a day old).

Leftover cooked rice is just perfect for making onigiri (see page 56). Simply reheat the rice in the microwave and mix the with your favourite flavourings and a few other ingredients, and mould together into bite-sized balls or triangles. It makes for a very quick, convenient and tasty snack!

Alternatively, if you need something more filling, stir-fry leftover cooked rice with some vegetables, or add it to a soup for a quick and comforting meal.

Leftover cooked rice will also keep for up to a month in the freezer – which is useful for busy people. Wrap it with clingfilm/plastic wrap while it's still warm in a squarish shape about 2-cm/¾-inch thick, so it will be easier to store and defrost. After it has cooled down put it in the freezer. Just put it in the microwave or steamer and make sure it is piping hot all the way through before eating.

You should avoid leaving cooked rice at room temperature for more than 1 hour and always use leftover rice that has been kept in the fridge no later than the next day.

SAKE

WHAT IS SAKE?

Sake is a fermented alcoholic beverage made from rice, water, koji mould and yeast. As rice has been central to Japanese diets for thousands of years, it is only natural that this alcoholic beverage is the national drink of Japan!

Sake itself has been around for over 2,500 years. It's not hard to tell why it became so popular when you consider the mass production of rice combined with our love of using the fermentation culture kojii (also used to make miso, soy sauce and pickles).

Over the years, Japanese sake has been produced at temples, by the government and by people in their own homes, but now it is most commonly produced in breweries. As beer and wine have become more popular in Japan, the number of breweries has dwindled slightly. However, it is still the go-to traditional drink of choice for formal occasions and celebrations, and will forever have a deep-rooted place in our culture.

Happily, the rest of the world is becoming more aware of the delights of sake, and you can now find it in supermarkets/grocery stores, restaurants, bars and even breweries around the globe.

It is often pronounced 'SAH-ki' by English speakers, yet in Japanese, the pronunciation is closer to 'SAH-KEH'. The Japanese word 'sake' simply means any type of 'alcoholic beverage'. So if you are ordering sake at a bar or restaurant in Japan, it is safer to specify 'nihon-shu', which literally means 'the liquor of Japan' or the more official term 'seishu', which is usually found on the label of bottles.

HOW TO ENJOY SAKE

PLAY WITH TEMPERATURE

Sake can be drunk at a wide range of temperatures. Even a small change in temperature can result in a different colour and allow for different flavours to shine through. The main rule, though, is to never drink premium sake hot, as this will spoil the flavour.

CHOOSE YOUR SAKE WARE

If you visit a typical 'izakaya' or sake gastropub in Japan, and order a carafe of sake, the waiter will bring you a tray full of different 'o-choko' sake cups, and you will get to choose your favourite to drink the sake from. O-choko are made from various materials such as ceramic, earthenware, lacquerware and glass, and come in many shapes and sizes. You can collect your own sake ware to maximize the enjoyment of sake in your own home.

EXPERIMENT WITH FOOD PAIRINGS

Sake is delicious when paired with many types of food, not just sushi! With its unique characteristics of gentle acidity, clean flavours and a great amount of umami, it goes particularly well with any delicate flavoured dishes such as fresh seafood platters and vegetable salads. Also, it is a great match for umami-ful dishes such as mushrooms or cheese and its clean acidity cuts through oily tempura or spice very well, too. Hot sake is great in the winter with a hot pot or similar warming dish, and cold sake is refreshing with summery dishes.

COOKING WITH SAKE

Just like wine, sake can be enjoyed both as an alcoholic drink and used as a valuable cooking ingredient. As part of the 'holy trinity' of Japanese flavourings (mirin, sake and soy sauce), it is used to season many of the dishes in this book. It is particularly good in stews, soups and sticky marinades. It removes strong smells from fish, seafood and meat but also helps other flavours in the dish to penetrate. If you aren't sure which sake to use in your recipe, buy basic quality sake and save the good stuff for drinking! Specialist cooking sake is available (just like cooking wine), which is normally seasoned with 2% salt. All sake contains a fairly high percentage of alcohol, which needs to be cooked off first before being used.

WHICH SAKE TO CHOOSE?

FUTSU-SHU 普通酒
This translates as 'regular sake' and it makes up 70% of products available on the market. It has a higher addition of other ingredients, such as brewer's alcohol and amino acid, and no minimum rice polishing requirement. Generally the more the rice is polished, the higher the grade of sake.

JUNMAI 純米
Junmai often has a round, full body and more complex style, with cereal or steamed rice-driven notes and a richer umami and acidity. It can be enjoyed warm or hot. Try this if you like Chardonnay or Pinot Noir.

JUNMAI DAIGINJO/DAIGINJO 純米大吟醸／大吟醸
This premium sake is extremely elegant, pure and smooth, with light to medium body. It is less umami but very aromatic, with fruity flavours such as melon, green apple, pear, tropical fruits and ripe banana. Try this if you like Sauvignon Blanc or Viognier.

JUNMAI GINJO/GINJO 純米吟醸／吟醸
This modern variety of sake tends to be lighter, crisp and refreshing. It is enjoyable well-chilled. Try this if you like Chenin Blanc or dry Riesling.

HONJOZO 本醸造
This sake has a small amount of brewer's distilled alcohol added at the final stage of brewing, which makes it lighter in umami and acidity, cleaner, crisper and drier in style. It can be enjoyed warm.

Other label terms:
KIMOTO/YAMAHAI 生酛/山廃
This is a special label term for sake made using the natural method for yeast cultivation. Kimoto or Yamahai labels often have deeper and richer flavours with more acidity, and tend to have more aging potential than sake made in the regular way. Try this if you like natural wine.

NIGORI/CLOUDY にごり酒
This style of sake is cloudy and milky in colour due to a coarse filtration process. Normally, it has slightly sweeter flavours and a creamier texture due to the remnants of rice sediments. It works well paired with light desserts or mixed with tonic water to make a refreshing cocktail.

SPARKLING SAKE スパークリング酒
Though this is still a very new emerging category (only about 20 years old), it is exciting to see sake with bubbles! There are various styles of sparkling sake available; from clear and light to heavy and from sweet to dry in style. The bubbles can be made with second bottle fermentation or an injection of CO_2.

TARU-ZAKE 樽酒
Until the early 19th century, when the very first glass vessels were used for sake bottles, all sake was made and stored in wooden vats, barrels or casks, mostly made from Japanese cedar woods. Taru-zake is a revival of this process where the sake is stored in Japanese cedar casks for 10 days or so to develop the spicy and pungent cedar wood aromas. It is great to drink alongside a platter of sashimi or sushi.

KOSHU 古酒
Most sake does not age well and would ideally be consumed within a year of being released from a brewery. This is when the delicate aromas and fresh flavours of sake are at their best. Koshu is quite a different style, and can be aged for extensive periods of time – usually 2 years or longer. Due to oxidation and the Maillard reaction (where the amino acid and sugar in sake caramelize in the bottle), this sake develops deeper colours such as gold, amber or even brown, and richer intense flavours of nuts, toffee, cheese or soy sauce, almost resembling Oloroso sherry. It is an incredible digestive drink and enjoyable when paired with cheese or chocolate.

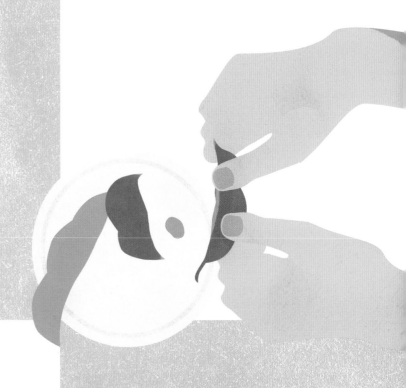

SMALL DISHES FOR SHARING

CHAWANMUSHI
STEAMED SAVOURY EGG CUSTARDS

It is said that the standard of a French restaurant can be determined by the quality of its French onion soup, the main component of which is a rich and freshly-made stock. High-quality establishments will use this delicious stock as a base in many other dishes.

Chawanmushi is an ancient Japanese dish that literally translates to steamed (mushi) teacup (chawan). Similarly to French onion soup, Japanese dashi stock is one of the few main ingredients here, so it is no surprise that it is served in many Japanese fine dining restaurants to show off the skills of the chef. If you get it right, the high liquid-to-egg ratio and the lack of milk or cream, makes it the lightest and silkiest recipe for egg custard you'll ever have!

4 king prawns/jumbo shrimp, peeled and deveined (though you can leave tails on for decoration if liked)
4 x 80 g/3 oz. pieces of firm white fish such as sea bass, sea bream, cod or haddock
a pinch of sea salt
2 fresh shiitake mushrooms

EGG CUSTARD
3 UK large/US extra-large eggs
400 ml/1⅔ cups cold Kombu & Katsuobushi Dashi (see page 24)
½ tsp sea salt
1 tsp light soy sauce
1 tsp mirin

TO GARNISH
4–6 pieces of carrot, peeled and cut into leaf shapes
2 tsp salmon roe
2 sprigs of coriander/cilantro

4–6 ceramic heatproof cups or ramekins with a 150–200 ml/⅔–generous ¾ cup capacity
bamboo or metal steamer

SERVES 4–6
AS AN APPETIZER

Dice the prawns/shrimp and fish into bite-sized pieces. Place in a bowl, sprinkle with the salt and set aside.

Remove and discard the stems from the shiitake mushrooms and cut them into quarters. Set aside.

To make the custard, break the eggs into a large bowl. Add the dashi, salt, light soy sauce and mirin. Mix well until the salt has dissolved. Use a fine-mesh sieve/strainer to strain the egg mixture, discarding any lumps.

Bring a large steamer to the boil. Meanwhile, divide the prawns, white fish and mushrooms between the bottom of each cup (filling up no more than a third of the capacity). Divide the egg mixture between the cups. Don't fill right to the top because the egg will rise slightly.

Carefully put the cups into the steamer (you might need to cook them in batches depending on the size of your steamer). Wrap the steamer lid in a small clean kitchen cloth, tying in a knot on top (to stop any water dripping into the cups) then place the lid on. Steam for 3 minutes over a medium-high heat or until the surface of the custards has each turned whitish in colour and set.

Carefully put a leaf-shaped carrot on top of each cup. Reduce the heat to low and leave the lid ajar as the custards steam for another 7–10 minutes.

Check if the custards are cooked by pricking them with a skewer. If clear liquid comes out, they are cooked, but if milky liquid comes out, then steam for a little longer.

Carefully remove the cups from the steamer with oven gloves. Leave for 5–10 minutes to cool down a little.

Serve the chawanmushi warm or cold. Garnish with salmon roe and coriander/cilantro and use a spoon to eat.

NASU DENGAKU
MISO-GLAZED AUBERGINE

This traditional dish has found its way onto most modern izakaya and Japanese restaurant menus – that's how good it is. The sweet and savoury umami flavours coupled with the melty texture of the grilled aubergine/eggplant make it sublimely satisfying. You'll be surprised at how many of your guests will shun meat in favour of this dish! The best way to eat Nasu Dengaku is to scoop out the miso-caramelly flesh with a spoon. Eaten with a bowl of rice, it also makes a great meal for one.

2 aubergines/eggplants
4 tbsp toasted sesame oil
4 tbsp vegetable oil
1 tbsp crushed roasted
   hazelnuts, to serve

DENGAKU MISO GLAZE
5 tbsp brown rice miso
2 tbsp soft soft light brown
   sugar
1 tbsp mirin
1 tbsp sake

MAKES 8

Peel strips of skin off the aubergines/eggplants lengthways, (alternately leaving a strip, then peeling a strip) to create a striped pattern. Top and tail each aubergine/eggplant, then slice each one widthways into 3-cm/1¼-inch thick round slices.

Use a sharp knife to score a cross-hatch pattern onto each side of the aubergine/eggplant slices. This technique is called a 'hidden cut', and it helps the vegetables to cook quickly and lets flavours penetrate.

Preheat the grill/broiler to 180°C (350°F) or to the medium setting.

Place the aubergine/eggplant slices on a baking sheet and drizzle with the toasted sesame oil and vegetable oil. Grill/broil the vegetables for 15 minutes until lightly browned and tender.

In the meantime, make the dengaku miso glaze. Combine the brown rice miso, brown sugar, mirin and sake with 1½ tablespoons of water in a small saucepan. Simmer over a low heat for 1 minute, stirring with a spatula, until the mixture is combined and glossy. Set aside.

When the aubergine/eggplant slices are lightly browned and tender, remove them from the grill/broiler and spread the miso glaze on top. Return to the grill/broiler for 4–5 minutes, or until bubbling.

Sprinkle the aubergine/eggplant slices with crushed roasted hazelnuts to serve.

DASHIMAKI TAMAGO
ROLLED OMELETTE WITH RADISH GARNISH

Originating from the Kansai region of Japan, dashimaki tamago is a refined version of the famous tamagoyaki, literally meaning 'grilled egg'. The addition of the dashi seasons the egg to perfection. Even though the eggs are well-cooked, the texture of a good tamagoyaki should be soft and tender, like a soft-set French-style omelette. Traditionally, a Japanese rectangular or square-shaped frying pan/skillet (available online) is used for this recipe, but you can also attempt it with a round pan – your omelette will be more oval in shape and you may need to cut the edges to make it roll neatly, but it will still taste good! This is simple comfort food at its best.

60 ml/¼ cup cold Kombu
   & Katsuobushi Dashi
   (see page 24)
½ tsp light soy sauce
1 tsp mirin
a pinch of sea salt
4 UK large/US extra-large
   eggs
2 tbsp vegetable oil

TO SERVE
Tsuyu Sauce (see page 74)
grated red radishes
finely chopped chives,
   to garnish

chopsticks
square or rectangular
   Tamagoyaki pan (Japanese
   omelette pan) available
   online or a regular round
   omelette pan
paper towel or a bamboo mat

SERVES 4

Mix the dashi, light soy sauce, mirin and salt together in a cup until the salt has dissolved. Set aside.

Break the eggs into a large bowl. Use chopsticks to break the egg yolks and mix together thoroughly with the egg whites so no lumps of white remain. Pour the dashi mixture into the eggs and stir gently.

Place the omelette pan/skillet over a high heat. Put the vegetable oil into a small bowl and soak a paper towel in the oil. Use chopsticks to carefully spread the oil-soaked paper towel around the pan to lightly grease it. Make sure the pan is hot, then pour a quarter of the egg mixture into the pan, tilting it to evenly spread the mixture. Use your chopsticks to gently burst the bubbles that appear on the egg as it cooks. When the omelette is half-cooked (within about 10 seconds), roll it up neatly towards you using the chopsticks, then push the roll to the back of the pan.

Spread over another layer of oil in the pan using the oil-soaked paper towel. Pour in another third of the remaining egg mixture, tilting the pan so that the new mixture spreads out and under the first egg roll. Within 10 seconds, when the mixture is half-cooked, roll the first egg roll towards you so that the new omelette wraps around it to make one larger roll. Repeat this process twice more to use up the remaining egg mixture. Each time, try to spread the egg under the main roll as quickly as possible so that they stick together.

After the last roll, turn the heat off. Put a clean paper towel or bamboo mat on a plate and tightly wrap the egg roll in it. Leave for 3 minutes.

Unwrap the egg roll and cut into 2-cm/¾-inch thick slices. Serve warm topped with tsuyu sauce and grated red radishes, garnished with finely chopped chives.

YAKI MOROKOSHI
SOY-GLAZED CORN

Grilled sweetcorn brushed with soy sauce is a typical Japanese festival food, and sold by many street vendors throughout the country. The sweetness of the corn married with the saltiness of the soy sauce is a match made in heaven! Even the smell of it cooking is enough to make your mouth water. This recipe is so easy to make and perfect for a party.

2 sweetcorn cobs/ears
15 g/1 tbsp butter
2 tbsp soy sauce
2 tbsp mirin

MAKES 4

Steam the sweetcorn cobs/ears in a steamer for 7 minutes until just tender. Set aside.

Melt the butter in a small frying pan/skillet over a medium heat. Stir in the soy sauce and mirin and simmer for 1 minute, until thickened. Pour the glaze into a wide shallow dish (large enough to fit the corn inside).

Preheat the grill/broiler to 240°C (475°F) or to the high setting.

Roll the steamed sweetcorn in the glaze to coat on all sides. Place on a grill tray with foil underneath to catch any glaze, and grill/broil for 5 minutes, turning a couple of times, until the corn is evenly charred and browned.

Chop the corn widthways into portions and serve hot.

EDAMAME NO WASABI AE
WASABI EDAMAME BEANS

Seasoned edamame beans are one of the most common snacks at izakaya bars and this recipe is perfect to share with friends alongside a glass of beer. There is beauty in the simplicity of the classic salt-sprinkled version, but this recipe is great if you like a bit more of a flavour-kick or have some leftover wasabi at home that you don't know what to do with. I tend to keep a stash of frozen edamame beans in pods in my freezer for this easy to prepare, moreish snack.

500 g/1 lb. 2 oz. frozen
   edamame beans in pods
2 tbsp toasted black
   sesame seeds, to serve

WASABI DRESSING
1 tbsp wasabi paste
1 tbsp olive oil
1½ tsp sea salt

SERVES 4

In a large saucepan, bring 2 litres/quarts of water to the boil.

Meanwhile, combine the wasabi paste, olive oil and sea salt for the dressing in a bowl.

Add the edamame to the boiling water in the saucepan and boil for about 3 minutes until cooked.

Drain the beans and leave them to cool down. (Don't be tempted to mix the hot beans with the dressing, otherwise the wasabi flavour will be lost.)

Mix the cooled edamame beans into the wasabi dressing and sprinkle with toasted black sesame seeds to serve.

KOROKKE
POTATO & BEEF CROQUETTES

When the French croquette was introduced to Japan in 1887, the Japanese created their own version without dairy products (rarely used in Japan) replacing the béchamel sauce with potato. Thus, the korokke was born! You can now find this popular dish in many households and at deli counters across Japan. As I was making this recipe with beautiful English produce – it struck me – korokke are a bit like cottage pie, but in the shape of a fishcake. What's not to like?! These are great served as an appetizer with a fresh side salad.

600 g/1 lb. 5 oz. floury potatoes (such as Maris Piper), peeled and cut into quarters
1 beef stock cube
25 g/1¾ tbsp butter, diced
1 onion, finely chopped
125 g/4½ oz. minced/ground beef
1 tbsp sake
½ tsp sea salt
¼ tsp freshly ground black pepper
English mustard, to serve (optional)

CRISPY COATING
50 g/generous ⅓ cup plain/all-purpose flour
100 g/2⅓ cups panko breadcrumbs
1 egg, beaten
500 ml/2 cups plus 2 tbsp vegetable oil, for frying

TONKATSU DIPPING SAUCE
5 tbsp tomato ketchup
4 tbsp Worcestershire sauce
2 tbsp soy sauce
1 tbsp runny honey
1 tbsp date syrup

MAKES 6

Soak the peeled and chopped potatoes in a large bowl of water for 10 minutes to remove the starch, then drain well.

Put the potatoes into a saucepan, cover with cold water and crumble in the stock cube. Bring to the boil and cook for 15 minutes until tender. Drain well, then mash while warm with two-thirds of the diced butter. Set aside.

Meanwhile, place a frying pan/skillet over a medium heat and add the remaining third of the butter. When the butter has melted, add the onion and fry for 2 minutes. Add the minced/ground beef to the pan, breaking up the meat with a wooden spoon. Add the sake, then fry, stirring, for 3 minutes or until most of the meat has turned brown. Season with the salt and pepper. Add the minced beef mixture to the mashed potato and stir well. Divide the mixture into six portions, then mould each portion into small oval-shaped patties using your hands.

For the crispy coating, put the flour, breadcrumbs and beaten egg each into a shallow dish. Roll each patty first into the flour, then dip into the beaten egg and finally roll in the breadcrumbs to evenly coat. Sprinkle extra breadcrumbs on top of the korokke to ensure a thick coating. Refrigerate for 10–15 minutes to firm up.

Heat the vegetable oil in a heavy-based saucepan to 170°C (340°F) over a high heat. To check that the oil is ready, drop a few breadcrumbs into the oil. If they sizzle gently, then it means the oil is ready. Reduce the heat to medium to maintain the temperature. Deep-fry the korokke in two batches, for 2–3 minutes, turning over a few times, until browned and crispy. Remove with a slotted spoon and transfer to a cooling rack.

Mix all the tonkatsu dipping sauce ingredients together in a small bowl and serve with the warm korokke and English mustard for an extra spicy kick, if you like.

RENKON TSUKUNE
GLAZED LOTUS ROOT & CHICKEN MEATBALLS

In Japan, we call meatballs 'tsukune', which means 'to knead into a round shape by hand'. They are one of the most popular yakitori (grilled skewered chicken dishes) and I find them the easiest of all yakitori recipes to cook at home. This is probably because minced/ground chicken stays juicy and doesn't dry out quickly in the same way that whole pieces of chicken can do when cooked. The addition of the slice of renkon (lotus root) adds some lovely crunchiness, and finished with a glaze of caramelized teriyaki sauce, these are dangerously addictive.

250 g/9 oz. renkon (lotus root), sliced into rounds

3 tbsp katakuriko (potato starch) or cornflour/cornstarch

350 g/12 oz. skinless boneless chicken thigh fillets

2 shallots, finely chopped

½ tsp fine sea salt

a pinch of freshly ground black pepper

2 tsp peeled and grated fresh ginger

1 egg

2 tbsp panko breadcrumbs, plus a little extra if needed

4 tbsp fresh chives, finely chopped

2 tbsp toasted white sesame seeds

1 tbsp vegetable oil

TERIYAKI SAUCE

3 tbsp soy sauce

3 tbsp mirin

3 tbsp sake

1 tbsp soft light brown sugar

TO SERVE

shichimi (Japanese spice mix)

fresh egg yolk (optional)

large frying pan/skillet with a lid

MAKES 12 MINI MEATBALLS

Combine all the teriyaki sauce ingredients in a small bowl and stir until the sugar has dissolved. Set aside.

Lightly coat the renkon (lotus root) slices with katakuriko (potato starch) or cornflour/cornstarch on one side using a sieve/strainer (this will help them stick to the meatballs). Set aside.

Mince/grind the chicken thighs by pulsing briefly in a food processor (you don't want it super smooth) or finely chopping with a knife. In a large bowl, mix together the minced/ground chicken, shallots, salt and pepper so that the chicken is well seasoned. Add the ginger, egg, panko breadcrumbs and chives and mix well again to evenly combine. If the mixture looks too soft to be moulded, then add some extra panko breadcrumbs.

Using damp hands to stop the mixture from sticking, divide the chicken mixture into 12 portions and roll each portion into a small round ball. Gently press each meatball down onto the potato-starched side of a slice of renkon (lotus root), so that the mince is squashed into the holes. Flatten each ball to about 2 cm/¾ inch thick. Sprinkle the toasted sesame seeds over the meatballs.

Place a large frying pan/skillet over a high heat. Add the vegetable oil, then place the meatballs, renkon side-down, inside the pan. Reduce the heat to medium and fry the meatballs until browned on all sides. Reduce the heat to low, then put the lid onto the pan to steam the patties for 3–4 minutes.

Remove the lid and pour the teriyaki sauce over the meatballs in the pan. Turn the heat back up a little and simmer for about 3 minutes until it has thickened and glazed the surface of the meatballs.

Remove from the pan and serve the renkon tsukune with shichimi and fresh egg yolk for dipping, if you like.

KUSHIKATSU
DEEP-FRIED CRISPY SKEWERS

Skewered dishes are a very popular easy-to-eat izakaya bar snack in Japan. With a variety of ingredients on your skewers, every bite is different! They are delicious served with this goma miso sauce or with Tonkatsu Sauce (see page 46).

5 raw king prawns/jumbo
   shrimps
180 g/6 oz. pork tenderloin
1 red onion
½ courgette/zucchini
5 baby corn
2 hard-boiled quails' eggs
5 raw scallops
lime wedges, to serve

CRISPY COATING
100 g/¾ cup plain/
   all-purpose flour
2 eggs, beaten
180 g/generous 4 cups panko
   breadcrumbs
2 tbsp aonori (nori seaweed
   flakes) (optional)
750 ml/3¼ cups vegetable
   oil, for frying

GOMA MISO SAUCE
2 tbsp white sesame seeds,
   ground
4 tbsp red miso
2 tbsp soft light brown sugar
1 tbsp mirin
1 tbsp sake

20 wooden skewers

MAKES 20 SKEWERS

Prepare the skewer ingredients. Peel the prawns/shrimps, keeping the tails on but trimming the tails back by about 2 mm/⅛ inch. Devein the prawns/shrimp by inserting a skewer near the start of the tail and pulling out the vein. Slice the pork widthways into 1-cm/½-inch thick round slices. Cut the red onion into twelve wedges, and cut the courgette/zucchini into 1-cm/½-inch thick round slices.

Thread each baby corn lengthways individually onto skewers. Thread the quails' eggs and courgette/zucchini slices each onto separate skewers, lengthways, like lollipops. For the pork loin and scallops, skewer a red onion wedge first, then a piece of pork or scallop to stop it slipping. For the king prawns/jumbo shrimps, insert the skewer from the back of the tail through to the top in order to stretch the flesh and avoid curling while cooking.

For the crispy coating, place the flour, eggs and panko breadcrumbs individually into shallow dishes. If you are using the aonori, mix these into the breadcrumbs. Holding the ingredients by their skewers, roll in the flour to give a light coating, then dip into the egg, followed by the panko breadcrumbs, turning and lightly pressing down until they are evenly coated all over. Place on a large plate and refrigerate for 10–15 minutes to set the coating.

Meanwhile, for the goma miso sauce, combine the ground sesame seeds, miso, brown sugar, mirin and sake with 2 tablespoons of water in a saucepan. Simmer over a low heat for 2 minutes, mixing to a shiny paste. Set aside.

Heat the vegetable oil in a heavy-based saucepan to 170°C (340°F) over a high heat. To check that the oil is ready, drop a few breadcrumbs into the oil. If they float to the surface and sizzle, then it means the oil is ready. Reduce the heat to medium to maintain the temperature. Deep-fry the skewers in small batches of 2 or 3 for 2–4 minutes each, turning over a few times, until golden. Transfer to a cooling rack.

Serve the skewers with the goma miso sauce (or tonkatsu sauce) for dipping and lime wedges.

AGEDASHI TOFU
DEEP-FRIED TOFU IN TSUYU BROTH

These are little cubes of heaven when they enter the mouth: crispy on the outside, creamy on the inside with a dash of umami-rich sauce. The katakuriko gives the coating a distinctive soft, almost jelly-like texture when in contact with the tsuyu. And although it is deep-fried, it's hardly greasy as the coating is so thin. This can become seriously addictive. No wonder it is one of the most popular dishes ordered in izakayas. Even if you're not a tofu lover, you must still give this a try!

300 g/10½ oz. silken tofu (soft tofu)

500 ml/2 cups plus 2 tbsp vegetable oil

3 tbsp katakuriko (potato starch) or cornflour/cornstarch

15 small red radishes (or 15 cm/6 inches white daikon radish), grated and excess juice drained

1 tsp peeled and grated fresh ginger, excess juice drained

1 tbsp freshly chopped chives

TSUYU SAUCE

200 ml/generous ¾ cup Kombu & Katsuobushi Dashi (see page 24)

2 tbsp light soy sauce

2 tbsp mirin

SERVES 4
AS AN APPETIZER

Handling it gently (as silken tofu is fragile), cut the tofu into four pieces, then wrap in paper towels and leave for 30 minutes to remove as much excess water as possible. Do not skip this step as it will ensure a creamy rather than watery texture on the inside of the tofu and a properly crispy outside.

To make the tsuyu sauce, heat the dashi, soy sauce and mirin in a saucepan until warmed through. Set aside and keep warm with the lid on until ready to serve.

Heat the vegetable oil in a medium-sized, deep frying pan/skillet to 180°C (350°F) over a high heat. To check that the oil is ready, you can drop a few breadcrumbs into the oil. If they sizzle and float to the surface and sizzle, then it means the oil is ready. Reduce the heat to medium to maintain the temperature.

Coat all the sides of the tofu in katakuriko (potato starch) or cornflour/cornstarch. Gently put two pieces of tofu into the hot oil and fry for 1–2 minutes, turning once halfway through. The tofu won't turn golden because it is coated in the starch, but it should turn crispy on the outside. Remove with a slotted spoon and drain on paper towels while you cook the other two pieces of tofu.

Divide the warm tsuyu sauce between four serving bowls and then place a piece of tofu into each bowl. Top each piece of tofu with grated radish, ginger and freshly chopped chives.

ONIGIRI & YAKI ONIGIRI
FLAVOURED RICE BALLS

Onigiri are Japan's number one comfort food and they are most definitely my desert island dish. They're simply cooked Japanese rice moulded into triangular or round shapes and mixed with, stuffed with, or covered with delicious fillings or toppings. They make great appetizers or snacks and are perfect for a packed lunch or picnic. Grilled/broiled yaki onigiri are a step up from simple onigiri, with a crisp rice crust on the outside and a warm, fluffy inside. Here are some of my favourite recipes.

SMOKED MACKEREL & DILL

140 g/5 oz. smoked mackerel with black pepper, skin removed and flaked by hand
400 g/3 cups cooked brown Japanese rice
2 tbsp fresh dill, finely chopped
2 tbsp capers, drained and finely chopped
2 tsp light soy sauce

MAKES 4

In a large bowl, mix together the mackerel, cooked brown rice, chopped dill, capers and light soy sauce.

Divide the rice mixture into four, then shape into oval balls.

UMEBOSHI & CORIANDER

400 g/3 cups cooked white Japanese rice
4 umeboshi plums, pitted and diced
2 tbsp roughly chopped coriander/cilantro leaves
60 g/½ cup cooked edamame beans

MAKES 8

Combine all the ingredients together in a mixing bowl.

Divide the rice mixture into eight, then shape into large rounds.

WATERCRESS & SESAME

2 tsp toasted sesame oil
50 g/1½ cups fresh watercress, finely chopped
¼ tsp sea salt
400 g/3 cups cooked white Japanese rice
2 tbsp toasted sesame oil

MAKES 4

Heat the 2 teaspoons of sesame oil in a saucepan over a medium heat, add the watercress and cook for 2 minutes. Add the salt. Transfer to a bowl and stir in the rice and the 2 tablespoons sesame oil.

Divide the rice mixture into four, then shape into balls.

YAKI ONIGIRI WITH NEGI MISO

400 g/3 cups cooked white Japanese rice
4 tbsp grated Parmesan cheese
2 tbsp freshly chopped parsley
2 tsp vegetable oil

NEGI MISO SAUCE

100 g/3½ oz. red miso
1 tbsp soft light brown sugar
2 tbsp sake
2 tbsp mirin
1 egg yolk
20 g/¾ oz. leeks, finely chopped

MAKES 4

Preheat a saucepan over a medium heat and add the miso, brown sugar, sake, mirin and yolk. Lower the heat and stir for 2 minutes until the egg is cooked. Add the leeks and cook for 1 minute.

Preheat the grill/broiler to 200°C (400°F) or to medium-high.

Mix the rice with the Parmesan and parsley, then divide and shape into four rounds with two flattened opposing sides. Place the onigiri on oil-brushed foil on a grill/broiler pan. Grill/broil for 7 minutes, turn and cook for 3 minutes more. When crispy, spread the negi miso sauce on top of each onigiri, then grill/broil for a final 3 minutes.

CHICKEN KARAAGE
JAPANESE FRIED CHICKEN

Chicken karaage is so popular in Japan that many cities across the country host annual karaage festivals, with the pinnacle being the Karaage Grand Prix which decides on the best karaage of the year. The main difference between the distinctly Japanese karaage recipe and other fried chicken recipes is the marinade made from the 'Holy Trinity' ingredients (mirin, sake and soy sauce), as well as garlic and ginger for aromatic flavour, and a dusting of mixed katakuriko (potato flour) and plain/all-purpose flour before deep-frying. Thanks to this technique, the chicken retains its succulent taste, tenderness and crispiness even after it turns cold! This makes it perfect for a bento box lunch the next day.

6 free-range skin-on boneless
   chicken thighs
90 g/¾ cup tbsp katakuriko
   (potato starch) or
   cornflour/cornstarch
90 g/⅔ cup tbsp plain/
   all-purpose flour
1 litre/quart vegetable oil,
   for deep-frying

MARINADE
90 ml/⅓ cup soy sauce
45 ml/3 tbsp mirin
45 ml/3 tbsp sake
1 tbsp peeled and grated
   fresh ginger
1 tbsp peeled and grated
   garlic

SERVES 4–6

Put all the marinade ingredients in a large bowl and mix well to evenly combine.

Cut each chicken thigh into four pieces and add to the marinade. Mix well with your hands, rubbing the marinade into the chicken all over to give it a good coating. Cover the bowl with clingfilm/plastic wrap and refrigerate for at least 30 minutes or overnight.

Mix together the katakuriko (potato starch) or cornflour/cornstarch and plain/all-purpose flour on a plate. Drain any excess marinade from the meat and discard, then toss the marinated meat in the flour mixture to give a light but even coating on all sides.

Heat the vegetable oil in a heavy-based saucepan to 170°C (340°F) over a high heat. To check that the oil is ready, drop in a small piece of batter (made out of a mixture of the breadcrumbs and marinade). If it sinks halfway and then floats to the surface and sizzles, then it means the oil is ready. Reduce the heat to medium to maintain the temperature.

Deep-fry the chicken, 6–8 pieces at a time, for about 4 minutes per batch, turning over a few times in the oil until crispy. Cut the largest piece in half to check that the meat is cooked through. Remove with a slotted spoon and drain on a cooling rack or paper towels while you fry the rest. Serve warm or even cold the next day!

YAKI KINOKO
MUSHROOMS WITH BLUE CHEESE, YUZU PONZU & TRUFFLE

As far as vegetable dishes go, this is the most decadent recipe – a real umami bomb! Imagine the taste of a beautiful selection of Japanese mushrooms covered in melting blue cheese, turning golden under the grill/broiler and finished with a drizzle of yuzu ponzu truffle dressing... I promise you, you will have no leftovers for the next day!

320 g/11½ oz. mixture of fresh mushrooms (such as oyster, enoki, shimeji, shiitake etc..)
100 g/3½ oz. asparagus spears
1 garlic clove, very finely chopped
1 onion, thinly sliced
30 g/¼ cup pine nuts
1 tbsp vegetable oil
40 g/1½ oz. blue cheese

YUZU PONZU TRUFFLE DRESSING
3 tbsp Yuzu Ponzu (see page 128)
2 tsp black truffle oil
2 slices of peeled garlic

SERVES 4
AS AN APPETIZER

First make the truffle dressing. Stir together the ponzu sauce and black truffle oil in a small bowl. Add the slices of garlic and leave for the flavour to infuse until ready to serve. Remove the garlic before serving.

Preheat the grill/broiler to 200°C (400°F) or to medium-high.

Trim the mushrooms and remove the woody parts from the bottoms. Cut any larger ones into bite-sized pieces. Peel the bottoms of the asparagus spears and trim the ends off at an angle (so that they are about 3 cm/1¼ inch lengths).

Place the mushrooms, asparagus, chopped garlic and onion into a large baking dish. All the ingredients should be evenly spread out so that they can cook individually. Sprinkle the pine nuts and vegetable oil on top.

Put the baking dish under the hot grill/broiler for about 10 minutes, until the mushrooms are lightly golden. Remove the baking dish and crumble over the blue cheese in small pieces. Grill/broil for a further 3 minutes until the cheese is melted and bubbling.

Remove the dish from the grill/broiler and drizzle over some yuzu ponzu truffle dressing. Serve straight from the dish in the middle of the table with any remaining dressing on the side, and let everyone dig in.

HOTATE NO SASHIMI
CEVICHE-STYLE SCALLOPS WITH CITRUS SAUCE

Serving scallops raw as sashimi or tartare really makes the most of their incredible silky texture and elegant, sweet flavour. For this you have to get the freshest hand-dived live scallops in their shells from specialist fishmongers, or frozen sashimi-quality scallops without shells (available from Japanese stores). It would be a shame to do too much to the flavour of something already so exquisite, so in this recipe, I just dress them with a bit of yuzu ponzu sauce and yuzu kosho chilli paste, to add citrus and a little heat, and garnish with crispy spring onion/scallion and sea vegetables.

6 hand-dived scallops in shells, or sashimi-quality scallops

DRESSING
60 ml/¼ cup Yuzu Ponzu (see page 169)
½ tsp yuzu kosho chilli/chile paste

TO SERVE
½ spring onion/scallion
vegetable oil, for shallow-frying
dried mixed Japanese sea vegetables (such as wakame, agar, aka or tsunomata), soaked for 10 minutes in cold water to reconstitute, then drained
micro herbs (such as coriander/cilantro, purple radish), to garnish

shucking knife (if preparing the scallops yourself)

SERVES 6

Mix the yuzu ponzu sauce and yuzu kosho chilli/chile paste together to make the dressing. Refrigerate.

Cut out a 5 cm/2 inch piece of the white part of the spring onion/scallion. Thinly slice along the grain to make slender shreds of spring onion/scallion. Place 3 cm/1¼ inches of vegetable oil in a small frying pan/skillet over a medium heat. Add the spring onion/scallion shreds and let them shallow-fry before the oil gets too hot (otherwise they may burn). Start at a low temperature and let them cook gently for a few minutes as the oil heats up and they turn crisp. Drain on paper towels and set aside until needed.

You can either ask your fishmonger to prepare the scallops for you or you can do it yourself. If preparing them yourself, the shell should feel tight so you know the scallop is still alive. Insert a shucking knife in between the shells to make a lever. Put the shell down on a chopping board, then gently twist the shucking knife to prise it open. Run the knife underneath the scallop to separate its membrane from the lower shell, and with a spoon, scoop up the whole scallop. Remove the outer skirt and the roe by hand and discard. Remove the protuberant white bit of muscle stuck to the meat. You will now be left with just the nice round white scallop. Clean the prepared scallops and shells briefly in ice-cold water to remove any grit.

Place the scallops on a chopping board and score the cuts you are about to make around the sides with the knife blade held parallel to the board. Slice all the way through the scallop to make 8-mm/⅜-inch thick slices. One scallop should make 2–3 slices.

To serve, place some sea vegetables in each shell, top with 2–3 slices of scallop and drizzle with the dressing just before serving. Finish with the crispy spring onion/scallions shreds and micro herbs.

NITAMAGO & GYU TATAKI
MOLTEN EGGS WITH LIGHTLY SEARED MARINATED STEAK

If you're ramen-obsessed, you'll recognise these nitamago as one of its most famous toppings. But these molten marinated eggs are also delicious enjoyed on their own, or with some extra toppings, like in this recipe. Here, I have served them with gyu tataki (seared marinated steak) which tastes so decadent with the rich, creamy egg yolks. You can prepare the marinades for both the steak and the eggs up to two days before serving, which makes for easy dinner party prep.

4 eggs
2 tbsp soy sauce
2 tbsp mirin
4 tbsp Kombu & Katsuobushi
   Dashi (see page 24)

MARINATED BEEF
1 tbsp vegetable oil
250 g/9 oz. sirloin steak,
   (2-cm/¾-inch thickness)
1 shallot, thinly sliced into
   rounds
1 garlic clove, thinly sliced
2 tbsp soy sauce
2 tbsp mirin
2 tbsp rice vinegar
sea salt and freshly ground
   black pepper

TO GARNISH
fried shallots
baby cress

MAKES 8 HALVES

Bring 1.5 litres/quarts water to the boil in a medium-sized saucepan. Carefully lower the eggs into the boiling water with a slotted spoon to prevent them from breaking. Boil for exactly 7 minutes over a medium-high heat for the perfect soft egg yolks.

Meanwhile, combine the soy sauce, mirin and dashi in a large resealable plastic bag to make a marinade for the eggs.

When the eggs have finished boiling, immediately transfer to a bowl and run under cold water to quickly cool them down.

When cooled, peel the eggs. Place the peeled eggs into the plastic bag with the marinade, making sure the eggs are immersed in the liquid. Dip the bag into a bowl of cold water to remove any air and seal immediately so it is almost vacuum packed. Refrigerate and let marinate for at least 20 minutes, or up to 2 days, turning the eggs a few times to ensure even marinating.

For the gyu (beef) tataki, bring the meat to room temperature at least 30 minutes before cooking.

Heat the vegetable oil in a medium frying pan/skillet over a high heat. Season the steak with some salt and pepper on both sides, then fry for 1 minute. Turn the steak over, then cook on the other side over a medium heat for 1 minute for rare (based on 2-cm/¾-inch thickness of beef). Cook the meat for 20 seconds more on each side if you would prefer medium-rare. Wrap the steak in foil and leave for 2 minutes to rest.

Meanwhile, combine the shallot, garlic, soy sauce, mirin and rice vinegar in another resealable plastic bag. Drain away any liquid that has come out of the steak and add the meat to the marinade ingredients in the bag. Refrigerate and leave to marinate for at least 20 minutes, or up to 2 days.

When you are ready to serve, remove the steak and eggs from their marinades. Cut the eggs in half lengthwise. Very thinly slice the steak diagonally, then neatly place pieces of steak on top of the egg halves. Garnish with fried shallots and a sprinkle of baby cress to add a crunch and a peppery fresh flavour.

OKONOMIYAKI
SAVOURY PANCAKES WITH TOPPINGS

Okonomiyaki are probably one of Japan's most famous types of street food. The word okonomi means 'to one's liking', the idea being that you can choose your own toppings for these pancakes, a bit like a pizza. This recipe is based on the Kansai version, which mixes all the ingredients together, rather than the Hiroshima version, which layers them. It has taken me years of refining to perfect this recipe and I must say it is the BEST. I have taught it to many students, and now I can share it with you.

OKONOMIYAKI MIX

250 g/1¾ cups plus 2 tbsp plain/all-purpose flour

2 tsp baking powder

300 ml/1¼ cups chilled Kombu & Katsuobushi Dashi (see page 24)

4 UK large/US extra-large eggs

500 g/1 lb. 2 oz. green or white cabbage, finely chopped

4 spring onions/scallions, finely chopped

150 g/1 cup canned sweetcorn

20 g/¾ oz. yamaimo (Japanese mountain yam), peeled and finely grated (simply omit if you cannot find it)

vegetable oil, for frying

OPTIONAL TOPPINGS

4 very thin slices of pork belly (see Tip on page 99)

4 raw prawns/shrimp, peeled and deveined

1 fresh squid, cut into rings

100 g/1 packed cup plus 2 tbsp grated Cheddar cheese

TO SERVE

240 g/1 cup okonomiyaki sauce

180 g/¾ cup Japanese mayonnaise

20 g/¾ oz. katsuobushi (bonito flakes)

4 tsp aonori (nori seaweed flakes) (optional)

MAKES 12

To make the okonomiyaki mix, sift the flour and baking powder into a bowl and then pour in the chilled dashi slowly, stirring to incorporate and break up any lumps of flour. Don't overmix or the mixture will become tough. Refrigerate for 15 minutes.

Meanwhile, place the eggs in a separate large bowl and stir in the cabbage. Beat vigorously with a wooden spoon to create lots of fine bubbles and an airy texture. Gently add the spring onions/scallions and sweetcorn and stir in until evenly combined.

Remove the okonomiyaki mix from the fridge and mix in the yamaimo. Add the okonomiyaki mix to the cabbage mixture in three batches, stirring gently with every addition until combined.

Heat a large frying pan/skillet over a high heat. When hot, add enough oil to lightly coat the surface of the pan. Using a large serving spoon, spoon three batches of pancake mixture into the pan. Reduce the heat to medium, then scatter over your favourite toppings on the surface of the three pancakes while still wet. Cook for 2 minutes until small bubbles appear around the edges of the pancakes and the underneaths have turned brown. Don't press down on the okonomiyaki as they cook or they will become hard. Carefully turn the pancakes over and cook for a further 4–6 minutes, depending on thickness and what toppings you have used. Peek underneath to check whether the toppings are nicely cooked, then turn the okonomiyaki over again if you are happy and cook for 1 more minute on the first side. Repeat with the remaining mixture and toppings and serve immediately on individual plates.

For a nice decoration, spread okonomiyaki sauce all over the pancakes with the back of a spoon, then squeeze the Japanese mayonnaise over in parallel horizontal lines. Drag a toothpick through across the mayonnaise at intervals to create an attractive pattern. Sprinkle with katsuobushi (bonito flakes) and watch them dance as they wilt in the heat! Finally, sprinkle with aonori (nori seaweed flakes) for extra seasoning, if desired.

GYOZA NO KAWA
DUMPLING WRAPPERS

Gyoza dumplings are one of the most popular Japanese foods, although they actually originate from China where they are called jiaozi. The main difference is that Japanese gyoza are fried and steamed in a frying pan/skillet to become crispy at the bottom, hence their alias 'pot stickers'. I actually normally buy ready-made wrappers to wrap my homemade fillings, as when they are readily available it is the quickest option! However, if you can't find store-bought wrappers, or you fancy making your own from scratch, this recipe is surprisingly easy – just be sure to roll the wrappers as thin as possible, this is what makes gyoza so light and crispy!

200 g/1½ cups plain/
   all-purpose flour
a pinch of sea salt
100 ml/⅓ cup plus 1 tbsp
   boiling water
katakuriko (potato starch)
   or cornflour/cornstarch,
   for dusting

*8-cm/3-inch round cutter
(optional)*

MAKES 30 WRAPPERS

Sift the flour into a large mixing bowl and set aside.

Add the salt to the boiling water and mix well until dissolved. Add the salted boiling water to the flour, a little at a time, stirring with chopsticks or a spatula with each addition, until the mixture comes together. Use your fingers to combine well into a dough.

Turn the dough out onto a clean work surface and knead through for 10 minutes until smooth.

Wrap the dough in clingfilm/plastic wrap and rest for 30 minutes at room temperature.

Unwrap the dough and divide in half. Roll each half into a long cylinder shape (about 20 cm/8 inches in length), then cut each cylinder into 15 even pieces (each one should be about 9 g/¼ oz.). Cover the cut dough with clingfilm/plastic wrap or a damp kitchen cloth to prevent it from drying as you work.

Lightly dust your work surface with katakuriko (potato starch) or cornflour/cornstarch and press a piece of dough (cut-side face up) onto the worktop using your palm to flatten slightly. Using a rolling pin, roll out the dough to a thin circle. Cut out a perfect circle using the round cutter, if you like, and start to create a stack of finished wrappers, dusting the top of each with a little more flour before adding the next. Repeat the rolling and cutting process until all of the dough has been used. Cover with clingfilm/plastic wrap until ready to use. The gyoza wrappers will keep for about 3 days in the refrigerator and up to a month in the freezer. Defrost prior to use.

YAKI GYOZA
PORK DUMPLINGS

When we have gyoza at home, it becomes a family event. We make and then cook them straight away on the table (on an electric hot plate) and end up eating at least 20 each! I can't resist, especially with vinegar, soy and chilli sesame oil for dipping.

30 Dumpling Wrappers (see page 66) or store-bought wrappers

PORK FILLING
250 g/9 oz. Chinese cabbage, very finely chopped to rice grain size
1 tsp fine sea salt
250 g/9 oz. minced/ground pork belly
50 g/1¾ oz. spring onions/ scallions, very finely chopped
2 tsp finely grated garlic
1 tsp peeled and finely grated fresh ginger
1 tsp ginger juice
1 tbsp sake
1 tbsp toasted sesame oil
1 tbsp soy sauce
a pinch of black pepper
vegetable oil and toasted sesame oil, for frying

SU-JOYU DIPPING SAUCE
2 tbsp soy sauce
2 tbsp rice vinegar
2 tbsp mirin
4 drops of la-yu (spiced sesame chilli oil)

large frying pan/skillet with a lid, approx. 28–30 cm/ 11–12 inches

MAKES 30

Stir together all the ingredients for the su-joyu dipping sauce in a small bowl and set aside until needed.

For the pork filling, put the chopped cabbage in a large bowl, add the salt and mix well. Leave for 10 minutes to draw out the excess water.

Briefly rinse the cabbage in a colander, then squeeze it to extract as much liquid as possible.

Mix the minced/ground pork until smooth, then stir in all the rest of the ingredients, including the cabbage (apart from the oil for frying) until evenly combined.

Prepare a small bowl of water. Put 1 teaspoon of filling in the middle of a gyoza wrapper. Wet the edges of the wrapper with a dab of water. Fold the wrapper in half over the filling and make seven pleats where the edges connect, squeezing them together to ensure the filling is well sealed inside. Repeat the process for the remaining wrappers and filling.

When you are ready to cook the gyoza, heat the large frying pan/skillet over a high heat, then add ½ tablespoon vegetable oil and ½ tablespoon toasted sesame oil. Working quickly, put half the gyoza into the pan. Let them sizzle for about 2 minutes until the bottoms of the gyoza start to turn brown.

Pour 100 ml/⅓ cup plus 1 tablespoon of water into the pan from the rim, then quickly cover with the lid so that not too much steam is lost. Reduce the heat to medium and steam the gyoza for 4 minutes. The water will evaporate as the gyoza steam, leaving the bottoms crispy! Serve immediately with the su-joyu dipping sauce while they are still crispy.

Repeat the cooking process for the remaining wrappers and filling.

TOFU GYOZA
VEGETABLE & TOFU DUMPLINGS

Alongside running my cooking school, I also work as a food consultant for Japanese food brands to create some of their recipes. This particular recipe was developed for Yutaka's frozen vegetarian gyoza. My client wanted to have something unique to western market, so I added cooked quinoa and it produced Yutaka's original quinoa vegetable gyoza. I am very proud of it!

This recipe uses firm tofu rather than the soft type. To avoid having a watery taste, wrap the tofu in paper towels and put a weight on top to remove excess water. It creates a firmer texture. Add cooked quinoa to substitute renkon (lotus root) for a unique texture. It is perfect for vegans.

20–22 Dumpling Wrappers
   (see page 66) or store-
   bought wrappers
Su-Joyu dipping sauce,
   to serve (see opposite)

VEGETABLE & TOFU FILLING
125 g/4½ oz. firm tofu
120 g/4¼ oz. Chinese
   cabbage, very finely
   chopped to rice grain size
¼ tsp fine sea salt
2 spring onions/scallions,
   finely chopped
50 g/¾ oz. chopped frozen
   renkon (lotus root)
1 dried shiitake mushroom
   (soaked in a cupful of water
   for 30 minutes, then
   drained, stem removed
   and finely chopped)
1 tsp peeled and grated fresh
   ginger
1 tsp grated garlic
1 tsp light soy sauce
1½ tsp mirin
1 tsp toasted sesame oil
1 tsp stock powder (kombu)
¼ tsp fine sea salt

MAKES 20–22

For the vegetable and tofu filling, wrap the tofu in plenty of paper towels and compress under a heavy kitchen utensil for 30 minutes to remove excess water.

Meanwhile, put the chopped cabbage in a large bowl, add the salt and mix well. Leave for 10 minutes to draw out the excess water.

Smash up the tofu with a wooden spoon in a mixing bowl or use a food processor to break it up into a paste, then add to a large mixing bowl.

Briefly rinse the cabbage in a colander, then squeeze it to extract as much liquid as possible. Add the drained cabbage to the tofu along with the rest of the ingredients and mix until well combined. Use the filling to make and cook your gyoza following the instructions opposite on page 68.

Serve with the su-joyu dipping sauce.

EBI GYOZA
SHRIMP DUMPLINGS

Prawn/shrimp and coriander/cilantro is a well-known match made in heaven in terms of Asian flavour combinations. This recipe is not surprisingly loved by most of my students. It is preferable to use raw king prawns/shrimps in their shells for the best flavour instead of already peeled ones. Please be careful not to chop the coriander/ cilantro too finely, as it loses its unique flavour. When the these gyoza are cooked, you can see the vibrant orange and green colours peeking through the wrappers, which makes them so attractive!

20–22 Dumpling Wrappers (see page 66) or store-bought wrappers
Su-Joyu dipping sauce, to serve (see page 68)

PRAWN/SHRIMP FILLING
100 g/3½ oz. Chinese cabbage, very finely chopped to rice grain size
½ tsp fine sea salt
200 g/7 oz. raw king prawns/ jumbo shrimp, peeled and deveined
20 g/¾ oz. fresh coriander/ cilantro, roughly chopped
1 tsp peeled and grated fresh ginger
½ tsp katakuriko (potato starch) or cornflour/ cornstarch
1 tsp sake
1 tsp sesame oil
a pinch of fine sea salt

MAKES 20–22

For the prawn/shrimp filling, put the chopped cabbage in a bowl, add the ½ teaspoon of salt and mix well. Leave for 10 minutes to draw out the excess water.

Meanwhile, divide the prawns/shrimp in half and chop one half finely to make a paste (to bind all the filling together) and chop the other half roughly to add chunky texture. Place all the chopped prawns/shrimp in a bowl.

Briefly rinse the cabbage in a colander, then squeeze it to extract as much liquid as possible. Mix the drained cabbage and all the other ingredients into the prawns/ shrimp until well combined. Use the filling to make and cook your gyoza following the instructions on page 68.

Serve with the su-joyu dipping sauce.

SOUPS &
NOODLES

HIYASHI SOMEN
SOMEN NOODLES ON ICE WITH TSUYU DIPPING SAUCE

Somen noodles are the thinner Japanese version of udon (wheat) noodles. They are commonly eaten chilled during the hot Japanese summer, as they make a light, refreshing meal and cook in just 2 minutes. The tsuyu sauce takes a little longer, but this recipe makes more than you need, and it will keep refrigerated for up to a month. Tsuyu sauce is a concentrated all-purpose umami-rich sauce. It can be used thick for glazing, diluted 1:1 with cold water for dipping, or diluted 1:2 with hot water for soup.

300 g/10½ oz. dried somen
   noodles

TSUYU SAUCE
100 ml/⅓ cup plus 1 tbsp
   soy sauce
50 ml/3½ tbsp light soy sauce
100 ml/⅓ cup plus 1 tbsp
   mirin
50 ml/3½ tbsp sake
1 tbsp soft light brown sugar
5 x 5-cm/2 x 2-inch piece
   of kombu
katsuobushi (bonito flakes)

TO SERVE (OPTIONAL)
Tomato No Ohitashi
   (see page 159)
Age Bitashi (see page 167)
fresh lemon slices
fresh radish strips
peeled fresh ginger,
   cut into matchsticks
strips of dried nori
sliced blanched okra
sliced spring onions/scallions
diced cucumber
toasted ground sesame seeds

SERVES 4

First, make the tsuyu sauce. Combine both soy sauces, the mirin, sake and brown sugar in a small saucepan. Add the kombu and leave to cold-soak for 30 minutes.

After 30 minutes, place over a medium heat and start to bring to the boil. Just before boiling, carefully remove the kombu. Turn the heat down and add the katsuobushi (bonito flakes). Simmer for a further 3 minutes to evaporate the alcohol and dissolve the sugar, then turn the heat off. Wait until the katsuobushi (bonito flakes) sink, then strain the sauce through a fine-mesh sieve/strainer and leave to cool. Pour into a clean bottle and seal. Refrigerate until needed.

For the noodles, bring a large saucepan full of water to the boil over a high heat. Add the noodles and stir gently at the beginning to disentangle from their bundles. Boil for 2 minutes, adding some cold water if the noodles start to boil over.

Drain and immediately rinse the noodles under cold running water in a sieve/strainer to stop the cooking process. Drain well again.

Pull out small handfuls of noodles and curl/twist them into small bundles to stop them from getting stuck together in a big lump. Arrange the bundles on a large serving plate and nestle some ice cubes around.

To serve, dilute some of the tsuyu sauce with an equal amount of cold water and place into small individual serving bowls. Give each person a bowl of sauce and let them pick up bundles of noodles with chopsticks and dip into the sauce, adding fresh summery salad ingredients of their choice. The noodles should be slurped with a loud noise. It is not considered rude if you are in Japan!

4 MISO SOUPS

WATERCRESS TO ABURAAGE NO MISO SHIRU
MISO SOUP WITH WATERCRESS & FRIED TOFU

There are dozens of variations on miso soup, but I particularly love making this one when fresh watercress comes into season. It's a real celebration of nature coming back to life with the vibrant green of the watercress contrasting with mellow white miso. Aburaage (deep-fried tofu) brings a wonderful nutty flavour and adds a lovely texture to the dish.

½ piece of aburaage
   (thinly sliced deep-fried tofu)
800 ml/3⅓ cups Kombu & Katsuobushi
   Dashi (see page 24)
3–4 tbsp white miso
25 g/¾ cup watercress, leaves picked

SERVES 4

Rinse the aburaage in just-boiled water, then wipe dry with a paper towel to remove excess oil on the surface. Dry-fry in a frying pan/skillet (without adding any oil) until brown on each side. Dice into bite-sized cubes and set aside.

Bring the dashi to the boil in a large saucepan. When boiling, add the aburaage. Reduce the heat and bring to a simmer for 1 minute.

In a separate cup, stir the miso with a ladleful of the dashi until fully combined, then add to the rest of the dashi in the saucepan and mix in well.

Bring almost to the boil again, then turn off the heat. (Miso keeps its potent flavour and probiotic properties best when not boiled.)

When you are ready to serve, divide the watercress between your serving bowls, then pour over the hot miso soup. It brings out the wonderful peppery flavour of the watercress.

WAKAME TO TOFU NO MISO SHIRU
MISO SOUP WITH WAKAME & TOFU

The ultimate all-star Japanese soup recipe, this is served all around the world. In Japan, soups like this are traditionally served and drunk straight from lacquer bowls topped with lids, while the solid ingredients are eaten with chopsticks. Why not try drinking it the Japanese way?

2 tsp dried wakame seaweed
800 ml/3⅓ cups Kombu & Katsuobushi
   Dashi (see page 24)
100 g/3½ oz. silken tofu (soft tofu),
   diced into 1-cm/½-inch square cubes
4 tbsp miso of your choice (I use red)
1 spring onion/scallion, stem only,
   thinly sliced, to garnish

SERVES 4

Soak the dried wakame seaweed in plenty of cold water for 3 minutes, then drain well and set aside.

Bring the dashi to the boil in a large saucepan. When boiling, add the diced tofu, then reduce the heat and bring to a simmer for 1 minute.

If you are using a grainy miso, put the miso into a fine-mesh sieve/strainer and lower the sieve/strainer into the soup to let it dissolve. Discard any grains left in the sieve/strainer. If you are using a smooth miso (without grains), in a separate cup, stir the miso with a ladleful of the dashi until fully combined, then add to the rest of the dashi in the saucepan and mix in well. Bring almost to the boil again, then turn off the heat.

When you are ready to serve, divide the soaked wakame seaweed between your serving bowls, then pour over the hot miso soup. Garnish with the sliced spring onion/scallion.

RIKYU JIRU
AUBERGINE & SESAME MISO SOUP

This is another Shojin Ryori (Buddhist temple) dish. It takes its name from the historical figure Sen no Rikyu (from the late 1580s), the zen monk who perfected the tea ceremony and elevated it to an art form. Legend has it he loved the flavour of sesame, so you'll find a lot of sesame recipes are associated with him.

½ aubergine/eggplant
2 tbsp toasted sesame oil
800 ml/3⅓ cups Kombu & Katsuobushi
  Dashi Stock (see page 24)
4 tbsp brown rice miso
1 tbsp toasted white sesame seeds,
  to garnish

SERVES 4

Cut the aubergine/eggplant into 1-cm/½-inch thick round slices. If your aubergine/eggplant is very large, cut it in half lengthways first, then slice.

Heat the toasted sesame oil in a small frying pan/skillet and fry the aubergine/eggplant slices in batches until browned on both sides. Set aside.

Bring the dashi to the boil in a saucepan, then reduce the heat and bring to a simmer for 1 minute.

If you are using a grainy miso, put the miso into a fine-mesh sieve/strainer and lower the sieve/strainer into the soup to let it dissolve. Discard any grains left in the sieve/strainer. If you are using a smooth miso (without grains), in a separate cup, stir the miso with a ladleful of the dashi until fully combined, then add to the rest of the dashi in the saucepan and mix in well. Bring almost to the boil again, then turn off the heat.

When you are ready to serve, divide the fried aubergine/eggplant between your serving bowls, then pour over the hot miso soup. Sprinkle with the toasted ground white sesame seeds to garnish.

KAI JIRU
CLAM MISO SOUP

Sometimes the simplest dishes are the best, and this soup is exquisite in taste, yet humble in its components. Be sure to get the freshest clams you can though, as the beauty of this soup resides in the freshness of its ingredients.

200 g/7 oz. fresh clams in shells
15 g/3 teaspoons fine sea salt dissolved in 500 ml/
  2 cups plus 2 tbsp cold water (if using live clams)
800 ml/3⅓ cups Kombu Dashi (see page 23)
4 tbsp red miso
1 spring onion/scallion, thinly sliced

SERVES 4

Scrub the clam shells to remove any dirt from the outside. Clams bought from the supermarket will already have been 'purged' – had the sand cleaned out of them. If you have bought wild clams from a fishmonger, spread them in a shallow, flat container without overlapping. Pour the salt water over to just cover the heads of the clams. Cover with foil and refrigerate for 2 hours. The clams will spit out any sand inside. Rinse once more before using.

Add the clams to the kombu dashi in a saucepan, then bring to the boil. When the clams have opened, reduce the heat to low and simmer for 3 more minutes. Discard any clams that have not opened.

If you are using a grainy miso, put the miso into a fine-mesh sieve/strainer and lower the sieve/strainer into the soup to let it dissolve. Discard any grains left in the sieve/strainer. If you are using a smooth miso (without grains), in a separate cup, stir the miso with a ladleful of the dashi until fully combined, then add to the rest of the dashi in the saucepan and mix in well. Bring almost to the boil again, then turn off the heat.

Serve the hot clam and miso soup in bowls scattered with the sliced spring onion/scallion.

MISO SOUP WITH
WATERCRESS & FRIED TOFU

MISO SOUP WITH
WAKAME & TOFU

AUBERGINE & SESAME
MISO SOUP

CLAM MISO SOUP

KENCHIN JIRU
JAPANESE BUDDHIST VEGETABLE & TOFU SOUP

This recipe is from my great teacher Mari Fujii who taught me Shojin Ryori (Buddhist temple cuisine). Like all Shojin Ryori dishes, this is vegan, but if you're not a fan of the 'v' word, don't let this deter you. It is a really hearty, comforting soup on a wintry day, but it won't weigh on your stomach for hours. I find crushing the tofu in by hand at the end so satisfying. The story goes that several centuries ago, a young monk dropped a fresh block of tofu onto the kitchen floor. The floor was kept clean, so they added the smashed tofu into the evening soup rather than waste it. This became the same nutritious recipe that you see today!

½ konnyaku block, about 100 g/3½ oz.

1 tsp sea salt

½ slice of aburaage (thinly sliced deep-fried tofu)

1½ tbsp toasted sesame oil

1 carrot, peeled and chopped into rounds

10 cm/4 inches renkon (lotus root), peeled and chopped into bite-sized pieces

100 g/3½ oz. sweet potato, peeled and chopped into bite-sized pieces

100 g/3½ oz. daikon radish, or turnip, peeled and chopped into bite-sized pieces

3 shiitake mushrooms leftover from making the dashi, cut into bite-sized pieces

4 tbsp soy sauce

800 ml/3⅓ cups Kombu & Shiitake Dashi (see page 24)

2 tbsp sake

200 g/7 oz. firm tofu

16 mangetout/snow peas, trimmed and cut in half diagonally

SERVES 4

Boil the konnyaku in water with the 1 teaspoon salt for 3 minutes to remove the smell. Drain and leave to cool, then cut into small pieces with a teaspoon to create an uneven surface, which will absorb more of the flavours. Set aside.

Rinse the aburaage in just-boiled water, then wipe dry with a paper towel to remove the excess oil on the surface. Cut into bite-sized pieces.

Add the toasted sesame oil to a large saucepan over a medium heat. Fry the chopped carrot, renkon (lotus root), sweet potato, daikon radish and konnyaku for 2 minutes. Stir in the shiitake and aburaage and let the oil coat all the ingredients. Add 2 tablespoons of the soy sauce to season.

Pour in the dashi and bring to the boil with the lid on.

Once boiling, add the sake and the remaining 2 tablespoons of soy sauce. Turn down the heat, cover with the lid again and simmer for a final 20 minutes until the vegetables are tender and cooked through.

When ready to serve, crush up the tofu by hand and add with the mangetout/snow peas to the soup. Stir and bring to the boil again to serve hot.

TONYU KINOKO JIRU
MUSHROOM & SOY MILK SOUP

This is a Japanese take on the comforting Western classic, cream of mushroom soup. Even if you think the original recipe can't be beaten, give this version a try. The use of kombu and shiitake dashi with the addition of miso makes it umami-packed and totally moreish. Replacing heavy dairy cream with soy milk makes the dish lighter, though it is full of protein so you won't be feeling hungry after a bowl.

600 ml/2½ cups Kombu &
  Shiitake Dashi (see page 24)
90 g/3¼ oz. mixed fresh
  Japanese mushrooms,
  (such as shiitake, shimeji
  and enoki), cut into
  bite-sized pieces
1½ tbsp sake
6 tbsp white miso
500 ml/2 cups plus 2 tbsp
  unsweetened soy milk
1 tbsp freshly chopped chives,
  to serve (optional)

SERVES 6

Pour the dashi into a large saucepan and bring to the boil. When it starts boiling, skim the scum off the surface of the dashi with a spoon.

Add the mixed fresh mushrooms and the sake. Turn down the heat to medium and simmer, uncovered, for 5 minutes.

In a separate cup, stir the miso with a ladleful of the dashi until fully combined, then add to the rest of the dashi in the saucepan and mix in well.

Add the soy milk and heat gently, stirring, until the soup is nice and hot but not boiling (boiling it will curdle the soy milk).

Pour into bowls and serve the creamy mushroom soup sprinkled with chopped chives, if you like.

TONKOTSU RAMEN
RAMEN NOODLES IN PORK BROTH WITH CHAR SIU PORK

Ramen is a noodle dish that has taken the world by storm. Tonkotsu ramen comes from Kyushu, my region, and the first thing I do when I go back home is have a big bowl of it. This recipe is time-consuming but worth the effort! You can make both the stock and the marinade a day in advance and keep them refrigerated.

CHAR SIU PORK
1.5 kg/3 lb. 5 oz. pork belly, skin removed
10 g/¼ oz. fresh ginger, unpeeled, sliced
10 cm/4 inches leek, green part only (or 2 spring onions/scallions)
200 ml/generous ¾ cup soy sauce
100 ml/⅓ cup plus 1 tbsp sake
50 ml/3½ tbsp mirin
2 tbsp soft light brown sugar
2 tbsp rice vinegar

PORK STOCK
1.25 kg/2¾ lb. pork shoulder bones
1 large onion, peeled and cut in half
1 carrot, unpeeled, diced
20 g/¾ oz. fresh ginger, unpeeled, thinly sliced
2 garlic cloves, peeled and left whole

SOUP
1.2 litres/quarts pork stock (see below left)
1 tsp fine sea salt
60 ml/¼ cup Char Siu Pork sauce (see left)
2 tsp light soy sauce
4 x portions dried ramen noodles, cooked following the packet instructions until al dente, then drained

OPTIONAL TOPPINGS
4 Nitamago Eggs (see page 62), halved
2 spring onions/scallions, thinly sliced
1 tbsp toasted white sesame seeds
2 tsp grated garlic
2 dried wood ear mushrooms, soaked in water for 10 minutes, well drained and sliced
20 g/¾ oz. pickled ginger
1 sheet nori seaweed, cut into squares

kitchen string

SERVES 4

For the char siu pork, roll the meat into a cylindrical shape and secure tightly with kitchen string. Transfer to a medium saucepan and cover with cold water. Add the ginger and leek, then bring to the boil. Reduce the heat, cover with a lid and simmer for 40 minutes.

Remove the pork from the pan and set aside. Keep 500 ml/2 cups of cooking water in the pan (discarding excess), then add the soy sauce, sake, mirin, brown sugar and rice vinegar. Return the pork to the pan, cover and cook over a low heat for 2 hours.

Place the pork and sauce in a suitable container, ensuring it is covered with the sauce. Let cool, then refrigerate and marinate overnight. The pork will keep this way for up to 1 week until you are ready to serve.

For the pork stock, boil the bones in a large saucepan with 3 litres/quarts of water for 10 minutes. Replace the cooking water with 3 litres/quarts of fresh water. Add the onion, carrot, ginger and garlic to the bones, then bring back to the boil. Simmer gently, covered with a lid, for 8 hours for best results (6 hours minimum). Add roughly 2 litres/quarts fresh water every 2 hours, when you see any of the bones uncovered, the stock should turn milky-white. Strain the stock using a fine-mesh sieve/strainer and return to the pan over a low heat.

Remove the char siu pork from the fridge. Remove the kitchen string (save the marinade) and thinly slice the meat, ready to top the soup.

To the pork stock in the pan, mix in the sea salt, 60 ml/¼ cup char siu marinade and light soy sauce. Bring the soup almost to the boil again to heat through.

To serve, divide the hot soup between serving bowls and add the cooked noodles. Top with slices of char siu pork and a selection of other toppings, such as eggs, spring onions/scallions, sesame seeds, grated garlic, mushrooms, pickled ginger and nori seaweed.

BUTA JIRU
PORK & VEGETABLES IN GINGER MISO SOUP

Buta jiru translates as 'pork soup', but this is effectively a miso soup with lots of vegetables and a bit of pork. It has a much higher ingredient-to-liquid ratio than traditional miso soup (predominantly liquid), which makes it very filling and satisfying despite being low in calories. It is important to use pork belly, a cut of meat high in collagen and rich in flavour, as this enhances the already umami-packed dashi. The pork meat should also be thinly sliced so that it cooks quickly in the broth. Freshly grated ginger added right at the end gives this soup a real punch of spicy flavour.

1 tbsp vegetable oil
1 carrot, peeled and sliced
   into rounds, then halved
¼ daikon radish or turnip,
   peeled and sliced
800 ml/3⅓ cups Kombu
   & Katsuobushi Dashi
   (see page 24)
100 g/3½ oz. pork belly,
   thinly sliced into 2-cm/
   ¾-inch length strips
   (see Tip on page 99)
a handful of beansprouts
12 sugar snap peas, trimmed
4 tbsp white miso
2 tbsp mirin
1 tbsp peeled and grated
   fresh ginger

TO SERVE
2 spring onions/scallions,
   thinly sliced
shichimi (Japanese spice mix),
   to taste

SERVES 4–6

Place the oil in a saucepan over a medium heat. Add the carrot and daikon radish or turnip and fry for 2 minutes.

Pour the dashi into the pan and bring to the boil. Once boiling, turn the heat down and bring to a simmer.

Add the sliced pork belly to the simmering stock, piece-by-piece, to make sure they don't stick together. Use a spoon to skim any scum from the surface of the soup. Cover with a lid and simmer for 7 minutes until the carrot is tender.

Uncovered the pan, then add the beansprouts and sugar snap peas and simmer for 3 minutes more.

Finally, mix the miso and mirin together in a cup with a ladleful of the dashi until well dissolved, then pour back into the soup. Bring back almost to the boil, then stir in the grated ginger and remove from the heat.

Pour into serving bowls and serve sprinkled with spring onions/scallions and shichimi spice mix to taste.

TEMPURA UDON
UDON NOODLE SOUP WITH TEMPURA

I always choose the tempura udon in noodle restaurants. I love the combination of the thick chewy noodles and the crunchy tempura in a simple soy sauce and dashi broth. Interestingly, the Portuguese introduced deep-frying vegetables and fish in batter to the Nagasaki region of Japan in the 16th century, and tempura was born!

4 shell-on king prawns/jumbo shrimp, tails left on but trimmed by 3-mm/⅛-inch

1 onion, thinly sliced into rounds

1 carrot, peeled and cut into matchsticks

½ aubergine/eggplant, thinly sliced into rounds

4 fresh shiso leaves

4 tbsp plain/all-purpose flour

500 ml/2 cups plus 2 tbsp vegetable oil, for frying

TEMPURA BATTER

1 UK large/US extra-large egg yolk

100 ml/⅓ cup plus 1 tbsp ice-cold water

30 g/3⅔ tbsp plain/all-purpose flour

20 g/scant ¼ cup katakuriko (potato starch) or cornflour/cornstarch

UDON NOODLE SOUP

800 ml/3⅓ cups Kombu & Katsuobushi Dashi (see page 24)

2 tbsp light soy sauce

2 tbsp sake

500 g/1 lb. 2 oz. dried or frozen sanuki udon noodles, cooked according to packet instructions

shichimi (Japanese spice mix) to serve

Insert a skewer near the start of the tails on the back of the prawns/shrimp and pull out the veins. Score lengthways along the underside and gently stretch them out on a work surface to prevent them from curling.

For the tempura batter, mix the egg yolk with the ice-cold water in a medium mixing bowl. Mix in the flour and katakuriko (potato starch) or cornflour/cornstarch using chopsticks or a whisk. Don't worry if the batter looks lumpy – not overmixing is key to crisp tempura.

Combine the vegetables and shiso leaves in a bowl and toss together with 2 tablespoons of the flour to coat. Coat the prawns/shrimp in the remaining flour.

Heat the vegetable oil in a heavy-based saucepan to 180°C (350°F) over a high heat. To check the oil is ready, drop a little batter into the oil. If it floats to the surface with a gentle sizzle, it's ready. Reduce the heat to medium to maintain the temperature.

Dip each prawn/shrimp into the batter and carefully lower into the hot oil. Deep-fry for 2–3 minutes. Drop a spoonful of extra batter onto the shrimps as they fry, then turn them over halfway through cooking. Remove with a slotted spoon and transfer to a cooling rack.

Pour the remaining batter into the bowl of vegetables and mix to coat. Use a slotted spoon to pick up some vegetables and let the excess batter drain off. Drop spoonfuls of vegetables into the hot oil and deep-fry in four batches for 2–3 minutes, turning a few times, until crisp. Remove and transfer to the cooling rack.

To make the noodle soup, bring the dashi to the boil in a large saucepan. Add the soy sauce and sake and simmer for 1 minute. Turn the heat down and keep the soup warm until needed.

Divide the cooked udon noodles between serving bowls and pour over the hot soup. Top with the tempura and sprinkle with shichimi to serve.

SERVES 2

YAKI UDON
STIR-FRIED UDON NOODLES

Udon noodles are thick wheat flour noodles, much more substantial than soba or ramen and definitely chewier! Their main attraction is known as their 'koshi-ness', the elasticity and bite in each mouthful! Although not the most common type of noodle in the West, in Japan they are as commonly eaten as pasta. Here they are stir-fried with pork, prawns/shrimp and plenty of fresh vegetables for a super-quick, delicious meal.

500 g/1 lb. 2 oz. frozen udon noodles

3 tbsp soy sauce

2 tbsp mirin

20 g/¾ oz. fresh ginger, peeled and grated

1 tbsp vegetable oil

120 g/4¼ oz. pork belly, thinly sliced into 3-cm/1¼-inch strips (see Tip on slicing meat on page 99)

40 g/1½ oz. prawns/shrimp, peeled and deveined

40 g/1½ oz. squid, trimmed and sliced into rings

1 onion, thinly sliced

½ carrot, peeled and cut into matchsticks

80 g/3 oz. Savoy cabbage, sliced into thin strips

80 g/scant 1½ cups beansprouts

1 tsp katsuobushi dashi powder

a pinch of ground white pepper

TO SERVE

2 spring onions/scallions, finely chopped

katsuobushi (bonito flakes)

1 tsp aonori (nori seaweed flakes)

SERVES 2

Defrost the udon noodles by immersing them in a bowl or pan of just-boiled water. Stir gently until disentangled and softened. Drain well and set aside.

Combine the soy sauce, mirin and grated ginger in a small bowl and set aside.

Heat the vegetable oil in a large frying pan/skillet (about 30 cm/12 inches in diameter is good) over a high heat. Add the pork belly slices and fry, stirring, until nicely browned. Add the prawns/shrimp and squid rings after about 2 minutes and halfway through cooking the pork.

Add the onion, carrot and cabbage to the pan and stir-fry for 3 minutes more.

Add the cooked udon noodles and beansprouts, then stir-fry with the vegetables for 1 minute.

Add the dashi powder and the soy sauce, mirin and ginger mixture and stir-fry just until all the ingredients are coated in the seasonings.

Finally, stir in the ground white pepper.

Divide the udon noodles onto plates, and serve topped with spring onions/scallions, katsuobushi (bonito flakes) and aonori (nori seaweed flakes).

PIRI KARA SOBA
SPICY MISO SOBA NOODLE SOUP WITH GINGER TERIYAKI TOFU

This dish is super healthy and quick to prepare, plus full of punchy flavours.
The perfect no-fuss meal for hungry people! Japanese cuisine tends to be mild
on the whole, but this dish has a real kick to it. The earthiness of the soba noodles
mixed with the chilli will lift your spirits and boost your energy on a cold day.

GINGER TERIYAKI TOFU
200 g/7 oz. firm tofu
1 tbsp vegetable oil
1 tsp peeled and very finely
  chopped fresh ginger
2 tbsp soy sauce
2 tbsp mirin

NOODLE SOUP
1 tbsp vegetable oil
2 garlic cloves, peeled and
  finely chopped
2 spring onions/scallions,
  whites only, finely chopped
800 ml/3⅓ cups Kombu &
  Shiitake Dashi (see page 24)
160 g/5½ oz. dried soba
  (buckwheat) noodles
3 tbsp red miso
1 tbsp gochujang (Korean red
  chilli/chili paste)

TO SERVE (OPTIONAL)
2 tbsp dried wakame
  seaweed, soaked in water
  to reconstitute, then
  drained
1 tbsp toasted mixed black
  and white sesame seeds
dried red chilli/chile strips
1 spring onion/scallion, thinly
  sliced

SERVES 2

For the ginger teriyaki tofu, wrap the tofu in plenty of paper towels and compress under a heavy kitchen utensil for 30 minutes to remove excess water.

Dice the tofu into cubes. In a medium frying pan/skillet, heat the vegetable oil over a medium heat and fry the tofu until browned on all sides. Add the ginger and stir in. Add the soy sauce and mirin and fry for 2 minutes until the tofu becomes caramelized. Set aside.

For the noodle soup, put the vegetable oil in a saucepan over a medium heat. Add the garlic and spring onions/scallions and fry for 1 minute to infuse some flavour into the oil.

Add the dashi and bring to the boil. Once boiling, turn down the heat and simmer for 5 minutes.

Meanwhile, cook the dried soba (buckwheat) noodles in a separate pan of boiling water following the packet instructions. Drain well and divide between serving bowls.

Combine the red miso and gochujang in a cup and stir in a ladleful of the dashi until dissolved. Add the miso mixture back into the saucepan with the soup and stir well to combine. Heat through for another minute, if needed, before serving.

Pour the hot miso soup over the cooked soba (buckwheat) noodles in the serving bowls, then top with the ginger teriyaki tofu, wakame, sesame seeds, dried chilli/chile strips and spring onion/scallion, if liked.

EASY ONE-PLATE MEALS

OYAKO DON
CHICKEN & EGGS ON RICE

Oyako translates as 'parent and child', which is a very poetic name for one of the most comforting dishes you will ever have. It is simply chicken and egg simmered in an umami-rich sauce atop some freshly cooked rice but, once again, simplicity rules supreme in Japanese cuisine. If you want to eat oyako don in true Japanese fashion, put down your knife and fork and use chopsticks. The secret is to start from the bottom, digging in to get chunks of rice to mix with the toppings and you will have perfectly balanced mouthfuls. Itadakimasu!

180 ml/¾ cup Kombu
  & Katsuobusi Dashi
  (see page 24)
2 tsp soft light brown sugar
2 tbsp mirin
2 tbsp soy sauce
1 onion, diced across the
  grain
2 skinless boneless chicken
  thigh fillets, diced into
  small pieces
3 UK large/US extra-large
  eggs

TO SERVE
400 g/3 cups cooked white
  Japanese rice (see page 29)
1 spring onion/scallion, thinly
  sliced
1 sheet of dried nori seaweed
pickled vegetables (optional)

SERVES 2

Combine the dashi, brown sugar, mirin and soy sauce in a medium frying pan/skillet (around 24-cm/9½-inches) and stir to dissolve the sugar. Bring to the boil, then add the onion and diced chicken. Turn the heat down to medium and simmer for 7 minutes, uncovered.

Meanwhile, break the eggs into a large bowl and lightly beat. Transfer to a pourable jug/pitcher.

When the chicken is cooked and the onion is softened, pour the beaten eggs into the pan, starting from the middle and pouring towards the outside edges in a circular, spiral motion.

As soon as all the eggs have been added, shake the pan gently to create a marbling effect between the eggs and the seasonings.

Reduce the heat to low and simmer for 2 minutes to soft-boil the eggs, then remove from the heat.

Portion some cooked rice into serving bowls and flatten slightly. Top the rice with half the egg and chicken mixture each. Sprinkle the bowls with sliced spring onion/scallion and tear up the nori sheet on top for some extra flavour. Serve with pickled vegetables for a refreshing crunchy taste, if you like.

Serve while the eggs still have a melting, soft-boiled consistency for the most authentic experience.

GYU DON
SIMMERED BEEF & TOMATOES ON RICE

Gyu don is one of the top five most popular donburi dishes in Japan, so I had to include the recipe in this book! It is basically a bowl of rice topped with seasoned, very thinly sliced beef and onion. It's simple to make and hits the spot magically when hunger strikes. Here, I have added some tomato to the traditional recipe for an extra layer of umami and a touch of colour to your bowl.

250 g/9 oz. sirloin steak
50 ml/3½ tbsp sake
2½ tbsp soy sauce
2 tbsp mirin
1 tbsp soft light brown sugar
½ large onion, cut into
   1 cm/½ inch wedges
5 g/⅛ oz. fresh ginger, peeled
   and cut into thin strips
1 large tomato, cut into
   quarters

TO SERVE
400 g/3 cups cooked white
   Japanese rice (see page 29)
shichimi (Japanese spice mix)

SERVES 2

Slice the sirloin steak as thinly as possible (see tip below) and set aside.

Combine the sake, soy sauce, mirin and brown sugar with 100 ml/⅓ cup plus 1 tbsp water in a medium saucepan and bring to the boil.

Add the thinly sliced beef, the onion and ginger to the pan and bring to the boil again. Skim off any scum that comes off the surface of the beef. Reduce the heat to low-medium and simmer for 5 minutes, uncovered.

Add the tomato and simmer for another 10 minutes, carefully peeling away then discarding the tomato skins as they soften and start to separate.

Portion some cooked rice into serving bowls, then top with the beef and tomato mixture. Add all the cooking juices so that the rice can absorb the flavours. Sprinkle with shichimi and enjoy.

TIP ON THINLY SLICING MEAT The easiest way to thinly slice a large piece of meat is to wrap it in clingfilm/plastic wrap and freeze for about 2 hours for a thickness of about 10 cm/4 inches, or a shorter time if the cut is thinner. You want the meat partially frozen, so the outside is firm and the inside is still soft. The texture should almost be the consistency of cured meat, rather than still frozen. This firmness allows it to be sliced much more finely. Unwrap the meat and thinly slice across the grain with a sharp carving knife for the most tender bite. Leave the partially frozen meat at room temperature for 30 minutes to thaw out a little before using, or place back in the freezer for when next needed.

NEVER NEVER DON
FERMENTED SOY BEANS ON RICE

With this dish, you will see whether you have true Japanese taste! The rice is topped with sticky natto (fermented soy beans), and in Japan we call this a 'neba neba' texture. The European husband of a Japanese friend of mine wasn't keen on natto and said he would 'never never' eat it. I renamed this dish 'Never Never Don' after him. Let's see what you make of it! To ease you in gently, I have added other toppings to give a pleasing variety of textures. The onsen tamago or 'hot springs egg' is an egg slowly poached in warm water, which gives a soft silky white and custard-like yolk.

2 organic eggs

4 okra

¼ tsp sea salt

2 x 40 g/1½ oz. packets
of natto (fermented
soy beans)

400 g/3 cups cooked
Japanese rice of your
choice, to serve
(see pages 29–30)

4 small red radishes,
very thinly sliced

1 ripe avocado, peeled,
pitted and diced

2 tbsp pine nuts, toasted

1 tbsp Tsuyu Sauce
(see page 74)

1 sheet of nori seaweed,
shredded

*20-cm/8-inch heavy-based
saucepan*

SERVES 2

To make the onsen tamago eggs, place 1.2 litres/quarts of water in the saucepan (this will be enough to submerge the eggs). Bring to the boil. Add 200 ml/generous ¾ cup cold water to the pan and turn off the heat.

Put the eggs in gently, then cover with a lid. Leave the eggs to slow-poach for 18 minutes in the residual heat.

Drain and then gently rinse the eggs under cold running water to stop the cooking process completely. Drain again. Set aside.

Place the okra on a chopping board and sprinkle with the sea salt. Use your palms to roll the okra in the salt, this will help to remove the hairy surface and makes the colour bright green.

Bring some water to the boil in a saucepan and boil the salted okra for 2 minutes. Rinse under cold running water to stop the cooking process and drain. Slice the okra thinly and set aside.

Stir the natto (fermented soy beans) inside their packets to create the 'neba neba' texture (almost sticky, slimy and stringy).

To serve, portion the cooked rice into serving bowls. Crack the shells of the onsen tamago eggs open and top each rice bowl with an egg, half the natto (fermented soy beans) and okra, radishes, avocado and toasted pine nuts. Finish with a drizzle of tsuyu sauce over the top and some shredded nori seaweed.

KATSU KARE RAISU
CHICKEN KATSU CURRY & RICE

Japanese curry is now a lunch favourite all around the world, but did you know that it was originally inspired by British curry? Curry powder was first sold in Chinese medicine shops in Japan, as it consists of many spices also used in traditional Chinese medicine. It quickly became a popular seasoning and is now sold in roux blocks and retort packages in supermarkets. 'Katsu' refers to the breaded cutlet also inspired by Western cuisine.

CURRY SAUCE
2 tbsp vegetable oil
1 onion, finely chopped
1 carrot, peeled and finely
  chopped
2 garlic cloves, finely chopped
4 tbsp plain/all-purpose flour
2 tbsp mild curry powder
1 tbsp garam masala
600 ml/2½ cups chicken
  stock
¼ dessert apple, peeled,
  cored and grated
1 tbsp soy sauce
2 tsp Worcestershire sauce
½ tsp fine sea salt
1 tbsp runny honey
a pinch of freshly ground
  black pepper

CHICKEN KATSU
4 skinless chicken breasts
50 g/generous ⅓ cup plain/
  all-purpose flour
1 UK large/US extra-large egg
100 g/2 cups panko
  breadcrumbs
1 litre/quart vegetable oil
salt and ground black pepper
800 g/6 cups cooked white
  Japanese rice (see page 29),
  to serve
parsley and cherry tomatoes,
  to garnish (optional)

SERVES 4

For the curry sauce, put the vegetable oil into a large saucepan over a low heat. Add the onion, carrot and garlic and fry gently for about 10 minutes until softened and lightly browned.

Add the flour, curry powder and garam masala to the pan and fry for 2 minutes until fragrant.

Turn off the heat, then pour in the stock slowly, stirring, to dissolve the curry powder (it may become lumpy if you add the stock too fast). Return to a medium-high heat and bring to the boil. Remove from the heat and blend the curry sauce with a hand blender or in a food processor until smooth.

Stir in the grated apple, soy sauce, Worcestershire sauce, sea salt, honey and black pepper. Place back over a medium heat and simmer for 10 minutes, stirring constantly, until thickened.

In the meantime, prepare the chicken katsu. Season the chicken breasts with salt and pepper. Prepare a shallow dish each of flour, egg (lightly beaten) and panko breadcrumbs. Coat the chicken breasts first in the flour, then in the beaten egg and finally in the panko breadcrumbs, ensuring the chicken is fully and evenly coated. Refrigerate for 15 minutes to allow the coating to set.

Heat the vegetable oil in a heavy-based saucepan to 170°C (340°F) over a high heat. To check that the oil is ready, drop a few breadcrumbs into the oil. If they float to the surface and sizzle, then it means the oil is ready. Reduce the heat to medium to maintain the temperature. Deep-fry the chicken breasts, two at a time, for about 5 minutes each (depending on the size of your chicken breasts), turning over a few times, until golden brown and crispy and the chicken is cooked through. Remove with a slotted spoon and transfer to a cooling rack. Leave to cool a little, then slice the chicken widthways.

To serve, place the cooked rice onto serving plates and pour over the warm curry sauce. Place the sliced chicken katsu on top of the sauce and garnish each serving with parsley and cherry tomatoes, if liked.

UME CHAZUKE
SALTED PICKLED PLUMS & RICE IN BROTH

This is a very traditional dish, usually served at the end of a meal. It's simple yet elegant and perfectly embodies Japanese washoku cooking. This particular recipe uses a very Japanese ingredient, umeboshi, which are tart and salty pickled plums. I like the honey pickled ones – they are less tangy and softer on the palate. In Japan, we say 'one umeboshi a day keeps the doctor away!'. Eat a little bite of umeboshi with each mouthful of this rice and soup.

8 fresh shiitake mushrooms
2 tbsp soy sauce
2 tbsp mirin
a pinch of ground sansho
   peppercorns or powder
600 g/4½ cups cooked
   Japanese brown rice &
   pearl barley (see page 30),
   to serve

SOUP
800 ml/3⅓ cups dashi of your
   choice (see pages 23–24)
1½ tbsp light soy sauce
1½ tbsp mirin

TOPPINGS
4 umeboshi pickled plums
1 spring onion/scallion,
   thinly sliced
¼ nori sheet, shredded
1 tsp white sesame seeds
wasabi paste (optional)

SERVES 4

Remove the stems of the mushrooms and discard them, then slice the mushrooms thinly.

Put the soy sauce and mirin in a small saucepan and bring to the boil.

Add the sliced shiitake mushrooms and sansho pepper, then simmer over a low heat for about 2 minutes until the mushrooms are caramelized. Remove from the heat and set aside.

For the soup, bring the dashi of your choice to the boil in a large saucepan. Once boiling, add the light soy sauce and mirin, then reduce the heat to low and simmer for 3 minutes.

Divide the cooked brown rice and pearl barley between serving bowls and pour the hot soup over the rice. Top each bowl with some mushrooms, one umeboshi and some spring onion/scallion, nori and sesame seeds. Add a little wasabi paste if you like it hot.

BUTA NO SHOGA YAKI
FRIED GINGER PORK WITH RICE

Alongside tonkatsu, buta shoga yaki or 'fried ginger pork' is probably one of the most common pork dishes made at home in Japan. As pork loin is a very lean cut of meat, it is important to use thin slices here (5 mm/¼ inch is the perfect thickness). When coated with this sweet gingery-soy glaze, the meat almost melts in the mouth!

560 g/1¼ lb. oz. pork loin
4 tbsp soy sauce
4 tbsp sake
2 tbsp runny honey
50 g/2 oz. fresh ginger,
    peeled and grated
2 tbsp vegetable oil
1 onion, thinly sliced

TO SERVE
800 g/6 cups cooked white
    Japanese rice
    (see page 29), to serve
4 portions of Kakitama Soup
    (see below)
red cabbage, finely shredded
watercress
dressing of your choice
    (see page 168)

SERVES 4

Remove any excess fat from the pork loin and thinly slice into 5-mm/¼-inch thick slices (see Tip on page 99).

Stir together the soy sauce, sake, honey and grated ginger in a small bowl to make a marinade. Place the pork in another larger bowl and pour the marinade over. Stir to make sure that all the meat is coated. Cover the bowl with clingfilm/plastic wrap and refrigerate for 15 minutes.

Heat the oil in a frying pan/skillet over a medium heat. Fry the onion for about 3 minutes until translucent. Add the sliced pork to the pan (reserving the marinade) and fry for about 3 minutes on each side until browned.

Pour the reserved marinade into the pan with the pork and stir-fry for 2 more minutes until caramelized and thickened.

Serve the hot sticky pork with cooked rice, kakitama soup and shredded red cabbage and watercress, dressed with your favourite dressing from page 168.

KAKITAMA JIRU
FLUFFY EGG & TOMATO SOUP

800 ml/3⅓ cups Kombu
    & Katsuobushi Dashi
    (see page 24)
1 large tomato, sliced into
    8 wedges
2 tbsp sake
3 tbsp light soy sauce
2 UK large/US extra-large
    eggs

SERVES 4

Place the dashi in a medium saucepan and bring to the boil. Once boiling, reduce the heat to low. Add the tomato wedges, sake and light soy sauce and simmer for 2 minutes.

Break the eggs into a jug/pitcher and stir well. Stir the soup, then slowly pour the eggs into the soup using chopsticks to stir the eggs in. Turn off the heat and serve the soup.

MAPO TOFU DON
SICHUAN TOFU & AUBERGINE RICE BOWLS

Many Japanese dishes are inspired by Chinese cuisine, and this particular dish originates from Szechuan, where at the end of the Qing Dynasty (1644–1912), the pock-marked (po) wife (ma) of a restaurateur became famous for her tofu recipe. Mapo tofu is soft and set in a spicy bean sauce and is traditionally made with minced/ground pork. It's a dish that goes particularly well with steamed rice – maybe that's why the Japanese love it so much! Szechuan spices can be very fiery to the point of numbing, so I've created a milder, but still fragrant version, using aubergine/eggplant instead of meat. It's just as soft but much lighter... guilt-free seconds are a must!

400 g/14 oz. packet of
   silken tofu (soft tofu)
1 tbsp toasted sesame oil
1 tbsp vegetable oil
10 g/¼ oz. garlic, chopped
20 g/¾ oz. fresh ginger,
   peeled and finely chopped
½ leek, thinly sliced
1 aubergine/eggplant,
   diced into small cubes

MAPO SAUCE
2 tbsp sake
2 tbsp red miso
1 tbsp mirin
1 tbsp soy sauce
2 tsp runny honey
1 tsp Sichuan broad/fava
   bean chilli/chili paste
½ tbsp katakuriko (potato
   starch) or cornflour/
   cornstarch mixed with
   ½ tbsp cold water
400 g/3 cups cooked white
   Japanese rice (see
   page 29), to serve
1 spring onion/scallion, thinly
   sliced, to garnish

SERVES 2

Dice the tofu into small cubes, then wrap in two layers of paper towels to remove any excess water. Set aside.

Meanwhile, to make the mapo sauce, combine the sake, red miso, mirin, soy sauce, honey and Sichuan broad/fava bean chilli/chili paste in a small bowl. Stir together and set aside.

Heat the toasted sesame oil and vegetable oil in a medium frying pan/skillet over a medium heat. Fry the garlic, ginger and leek for 1 minute to infuse the flavour into the oil, then add the aubergine/eggplant. Fry for 2 minutes until browned.

Add the mapo sauce and 80 ml/⅓ cup water to the pan with the vegetables, reduce the heat to low and simmer, uncovered, for 3 minutes.

Add the tofu cubes gently, then pour the katakuriko (potato starch) or cornflour/cornstarch and water mixture around the rim of the pan. Bring to the boil for about 1 minute to thicken the mixture slightly, then remove from the heat.

Divide the cooked rice between serving bowls and add the mapo tofu. Garnish the dishes with sliced spring onion/scallion.

TORI NO LIME TERIYAKI DON

CHICKEN TERIYAKI WITH LIME ON QUINOA RICE

Teriyaki is so popular now – you don't even have to go to a Japanese restaurant to have it. Supermarkets and grocery stores sell ready-made bottles of the sweet, soy-based glaze that you can use to marinate your chicken, salmon or whatever takes your fancy. But nothing beats the taste of a homemade teriyaki sauce. It is very easy to make, I like to add lime for an extra fragrant twist. After trying this recipe, you might never purchase ready-made teriyaki sauce again!

1 tbsp vegetable oil
2 leeks, chopped into
    2 cm/¾ inch lengths
500 g/1 lb. 2 oz. boneless
    skin-on chicken thigh fillets,
    diced into bite-sized pieces
4 tbsp katakuriko (potato
    starch) or cornflour/
    cornstarch

TERIYAKI SAUCE WITH LIME
3 tbsp soy sauce
3 tbsp mirin
1 tbsp soft light brown sugar
1 tbsp sake
1 tbsp lime juice and grated
    zest from ½ lime

TO SERVE
800 g/6 cups cooked
    Japanese rice & quinoa
    (see page 30), to serve
toasted white and black
    sesame seeds
yuzu kosho chilli/chili paste,
    to serve (optional)

SERVES 4

In a small bowl, mix together the soy sauce, mirin, brown sugar, sake, lime juice and zest to make the teriyaki sauce, stirring until the sugar has dissolved. Set aside.

Add ½ tbsp of the vegetable oil to a frying pan/skillet over a medium heat. Add the leeks and fry until lightly browned on each side. Remove them from the pan and set aside.

Place the chicken pieces in a bowl and lightly toss with the katakuriko (potato starch) or cornflour/cornstarch to evenly coat all over.

Add the remaining ½ tbsp vegetable oil to the same frying pan/skillet and fry the chicken, skin-side down, for 2 minutes until browned. Remove the pan from the heat briefly and remove the excess chicken fat by tilting the pan to the side and carefully soaking up the fat with 1–2 paper towels (taking care not to actually touch the surface of the hot pan with your hand).

Turn the chicken pieces over and cook for 2 minutes on the other side.

Add the leeks back into the pan, then pour over the teriyaki sauce, stirring to coat the chicken and leeks evenly. Simmer for 4–5 minutes over a medium-high heat until the sauce has thickened.

Divide the cooked rice and quinoa between serving bowls, then add the teriyaki chicken. Sprinkle with toasted sesame seeds and serve with yuzu kosho chilli/chili paste, if you want some extra heat.

CHIRASHI SUSHI
TOPPED SUSHI BOWLS

We make this dish at the end of our beginners cookery course to celebrate in style!
Indeed, chirashi is traditionally served on happy occasions and at parties in Japan.
Think of it as deconstructed sushi with colourful toppings. Usually it is served in
a big sharing bowl, but it also makes a great individual one-bowl meal too.

360 g/2 scant cups uncooked
   Japanese rice
5 x 10-cm/2 x 4-inch piece
   of kombu
1 tbsp sake

SUSHI VINEGAR
60 ml/¼ cup rice vinegar
2 tbsp golden caster sugar
1 tsp salt

TUNA FLAKES
60 g/2¼ oz. can tuna in oil
1 tbsp sake
1½ tsp soft light brown sugar
1 tbsp soy sauce

THIN EGG RIBBONS
2 UK large/US extra-large
   eggs
1 tsp sake
½ tsp golden caster sugar
a pinch of salt
1 tbsp vegetable oil

EXTRA TOPPINGS
250 g/9 oz. fresh sashimi
½ ripe avocado, peeled,
   pitted and diced
4 cooked tiger prawns/
   jumbo shrimp
4 mangetout/snow peas,
   blanched and cut in half
4 red radishes, thinly sliced
4 tbsp salmon roe
soy sauce

SERVES 4

Rinse the rice in a sieve/strainer under cold running water, mixing with your hands. Leave to drain and dry for 30 minutes.

Place the rice in a heavy-based saucepan with a lid and add 360 ml/1½ cups of water. (This is a little different from the standard ratio for cooking rice, as extra moisture comes from the seasonings. Sushi rice grown in countries other than Japan tends to be slightly drier, so if using this add 10% more water). Add the kombu and the sake. Bring to the boil over a high heat. When it starts to boil, reduce the heat to low and simmer for 12 minutes. Remove from the heat and leave for 10 minutes with the lid on. All the water should have been absorbed by the rice.

To make the sushi vinegar, combine the vinegar, sugar and salt in a jug/pitcher. Mix until the sugar and salt have dissolved.

Wet the surface of a wooden sushi mixing bowl (or use a wide shallow glass or ceramic dish) to prevent the rice sticking. Place the rice into the bowl and pour the sushi vinegar over, gently cutting and mixing the rice sideways with a spatula so that the rice grains don't break. Leave to cool for 20 minutes.

Meanwhile, for the tuna flakes, drain the tuna, reserving 1 tablespoon of oil from the can. Add the reserved oil to a small frying pan/skillet over a medium heat. Add the tuna, sake, sugar and soy sauce. Fry, while stirring constantly with four chopsticks or a whisk, for about 5 minutes until the liquid has evaporated to leave fine tuna flakes. Set aside to cool.

For the egg ribbons, break the eggs into a small mixing bowl and add the sake, sugar and salt. Mix well until the sugar and salt have dissolved. Heat a medium frying pan/skillet over a medium heat and wipe the pan with a paper towel soaked in the vegetable oil. Pour in a quarter of the beaten eggs, tilting the pan so it spreads evenly. After 30 seconds when the surface is cooked, turn over and cook for 2 seconds, then slide onto a plate lined with paper towels. Repeat to make three more thin omelettes. Cut the omelettes in half, then roll them up and thinly slice widthways into ribbons.

Divide the sushi rice between serving bowls and top with the tuna flakes, egg ribbons and any extra toppings of your choice.

OMURICE
OMELETTE ON CHICKEN RICE

Making omurice brings back memories of my school days. It was my favourite dish and the first thing I learnt to cook. I was obsessed with it! The typical way of making 'omurice' is to wrap the fried rice with the omelette, encasing it completely. It took me so long to master it to perfection: placing the omelette perfectly to wrap the fried rice. To make things a little simpler, I came up with the idea of an open omelette laid on top of the fried rice: the soft-cooked egg melting over the fried rice makes me even more mad about this dish. I hope you love this as much I do!

CHICKEN FRIED RICE

1 tbsp vegetable oil

2 skinless boneless chicken thigh fillets, chopped into small pieces

½ onion, finely chopped

½ carrot, peeled and finely chopped

20 g/⅛ cup fresh garden peas

4 tbsp tomato ketchup

1 chicken stock cube, finely chopped

a pinch of salt and ground white pepper

400 g/3 cups cooked white Japanese rice (see page 29)

freshly chopped parsley, to garnish

OMELETTE

4 UK large/US extra-large eggs

2 tbsp whole milk

pinch of salt and ground white pepper

20 g/1½ tbsp butter

SAUCE

4 tbsp tomato ketchup

4 tbsp red wine

4 tbsp chicken stock

2 tbsp Worcestershire sauce

½ tsp runny honey

2 teaspoons unsalted butter

SERVES 2

First, make the sauce. Stir together the tomato ketchup, red wine, chicken stock and Worcestershire sauce in a small saucepan. Place over a medium heat for 2 minutes to let the alcohol from the wine evaporate. Remove the pan from the heat, then add the honey and butter, stirring in until dissolved and smooth. Set aside.

For the chicken fried rice, put the vegetable oil in a large frying pan/skillet and place over a medium heat. Add the chicken and fry for about 4 minutes, stirring and turning, until brown on all sides. Add the onion, carrot and peas and fry for 3 more minutes. Add the tomato ketchup, chicken stock cube and salt and ground white pepper. Add the cooked rice and stir-fry until all the seasonings have been distributed evenly.

Divide the chicken fried rice between serving plates. Cover each portion of rice with clingfilm/plastic wrap (to prevent it from going cold and drying out while you cook the omelettes) and shape each one into a neat oval mound using your hands.

To make the omelettes, break the eggs into a mixing bowl. Add the milk and salt and pepper. Whisk together until all the ingredients are evenly combined.

Heat 10 g/2 teaspoons of the butter in a small omelette pan or frying pan/skillet over a medium heat. Pour in half of the egg mixture, tilting the pan to evenly coat the bottom. Immediately stir the egg mixture with chopsticks or a wooden spoon before it is cooked, this will ensure the even cooking of the omelette.

Just before the egg mixture is completely set, remove the clingfilm/plastic wrap from one portion of rice and cover the rice with the omelette. Repeat the process for the remaining egg mixture and serving of rice.

Pour the sauce on top of the omurice to serve and sprinkle with fresh parsley to garnish.

SPECIAL
OCCASION
MEALS

YAKINIKU
BARBECUED BEEF LETTUCE WRAPS

On special occasions, we often have yakiniku, Japan's very own Korean-style BBQ. This is for meat-lovers who also like a bit of spice and punch! Traditionally, we would have a grill on the table to cook the meat, and part of the fun even at yakiniku restaurants is that you cook your own meal at the table. However, it is just as good (and perhaps easier) to fry the meat in the kitchen and then serve at the table for everybody to make their own wraps, adding pickles and vegetables to their liking.

500 g/1 lb. 2 oz. thinly sliced sirloin or rib eye of beef (see Tip on page 99)
1 tbsp each vegetable oil and toasted sesame oil

YAKINIKU MARINADE
90 ml/⅓ cup soy sauce
60 ml/¼ cup mirin
30 ml/2 tbsp sake
1 tbsp runny honey
1 tbsp gochujang paste
1 tbsp peeled and grated fresh ginger
1 tbsp grated garlic
2 tbsp white sesame seeds
1 tbsp toasted sesame oil
1 tbsp vegetable oil

NAMASU PICKLE
5 x 5-cm/2 x 2-inch kombu
1 tbsp grated orange zest
75 ml/⅓ cup rice vinegar
2 tbsp agave syrup
½ tsp sea salt
250 g/9 oz. daikon radish, peeled and sliced into thin strips
1 carrot, peeled and sliced into thin strips

TO SERVE
4 Little Gem/Bibb lettuces
150 g/5½ oz. kimchi
8 fresh shiso leaves

SERVES 4

First, make the namasu pickle. Combine the kombu, orange zest, vinegar, agave syrup and sea salt in a bowl with 2 tablespoons of water and mix well to dissolve the sugar and salt.

Place the strips of daikon radish and carrot into a resealable plastic bag and pour over the vinegar mixture, making sure all the vegetables are immersed. Dip the bag into a bowl of cold water to remove the air from the bag. Seal immediately so it is almost vacuum-packed. Refrigerate and leave to marinate for at least 30 minutes before serving. The namasu pickle will keep, refrigerated, for up to 1 week. Drain before serving.

To make the yakiniku marinade for the beef, mix all the ingredients together in a bowl until well combined. Add the beef slices to the bowl containing the marinade and mix well to give an even coating. Cover and refrigerate the meat for a minimum of 20 minutes or overnight to let the flavours infuse.

Heat ½ tablespoon each of the vegetable oil and toasted sesame oil in a large frying pan/skillet over a medium heat. Using a slotted spoon to drain off excess marinade, add half of the beef to the pan and fry for about 2–3 minutes, stirring, until browned all over. Remove from the pan and keep warm while you fry the second batch of meat in the same way with the remaining oils. Reserve any leftover marinade in the bowl.

After cooking all the meat, pour the remaining yakiniku marinade into the pan and stir-fry until caramelized and thickened. Serve as extra sauce on the side of your dish.

Serve the yakiniku beef with the extra marinade sauce, Little Gem/Bibb lettuce leaf wraps, the namasu pickle, kimchi and shiso leaves.

NIKUJAGA
BEEF & POTATO STEW

Nikujaga is another dish that finds its roots in England. It even sounds the part, being more or less pronounced Mick Jagger! Literally translating as 'meat' and 'potato', nikujaga is a succulent slow-cooked beef, potato and noodle stew and now one of Japan's most-loved home-cooked dishes. At the end of the 19th century, admiral Heihachiro couldn't forget the taste of the beef stew he ate while studying in the UK, so he ordered his minions to recreate it. At the time, Japan had no butter or wine, so traditional Japanese seasonings were used instead, resulting in the dish nikujaga! In Japan, there is a saying that if the daughter can make a perfect nikujaga, her mother will tell her she is ready to get married... this tradition worked on my Italian husband!

650 g/1 lb. 7 oz. waxy
    potatoes (such as Charlotte
    potatoes or new potatoes)
180 g/6½ oz. fresh shirataki
    noodles
large pinch of salt
1 tbsp vegetable oil
1 large onion, sliced into
    wedges
2 carrots, peeled and roughly
    chopped into chunks
350 g/12 oz. thinly sliced
    sirloin or rib eye of beef
    (see Tip on page 99)
380 ml/1⅔ cups Kombu
    & Katsuobushi Dashi
    (see page 24)
2 tbsp sake
1 tbsp soft light brown sugar
4 tbsp mirin
5 tbsp soy sauce
16 mangetout/snow peas

*large saucepan with a drop-lid
    or a homemade drop-lid
    (see page 19)*

SERVES 4

Peel and cut the potatoes in half (cut any very big potatoes into thirds). Soak the potatoes for 10 minutes in a bowl of water to remove the starch. Drain and set aside.

Add 500 ml/2 cups plus 2 tbsp water to a small saucepan and bring to the boil. Add the shirataki noodles and salt. Boil for 3 minutes, then drain well. Set aside.

Heat the oil in the large saucepan, then fry the onion, carrots, and potatoes for 2 minutes, stirring.

Add the beef and continue to fry for 2 minutes, stirring, until the beef is browned. Add the shirataki noodles and the dashi stock, then bring to the boil. Skim any scum off the surface of the broth.

Once boiling, reduce the heat and bring to a simmer. Add the sake, brown sugar and mirin. Put the drop lid on, reduce the heat down to very low and let simmer for 15 minutes until the potatoes are tender and cooked.

Add the soy sauce, replace the drop lid and simmer over a low heat for 8 minutes. Finally, add the mangetout/snow peas and cook for 2 more minutes.

Remove the nikujaga from the heat, then cover and leave to stand for 10–20 minutes before serving.

This stewed dish always tastes even better the next day when the flavours have had more time to meld. Just reheat it until piping hot before you serve.

TORI NO NIMONO
SWEET & SOUR CHICKEN STEW

Stews don't always have to be winter comfort food. Reminiscent of an escabèche, this summer stew is very refreshing on a hot day, with its slightly vinegary sauce and its garlic zing, leaving you feeling nourished and satisfied without being too heavy.

8 chicken drumsticks
1 litre/quart boiling water
5 garlic cloves, gently crushed
120 ml/½ cup soy sauce
100 ml/⅓ cup plus 1 tbsp sake
80 ml/⅓ cup rice vinegar
50 ml/3½ tbsp mirin
3 tbsp soft light brown sugar
4 UK large/US extra-large
　eggs
cooked Japanese rice,
　to serve (see page 29)

*large saucepan with a drop-lid
　or a homemade drop-lid
　(see page 19)*

SERVES 4

Place the chicken drumsticks in a metal sieve/strainer. Pour the boiling water onto the chicken to rinse and pre-cook the surfaces (do this in two batches with two lots of boiling water if your sieve/strainer is smaller).

In the large saucepan, combine 100 ml/⅓ cup plus 1 tbsp fresh water with the crushed garlic cloves, soy sauce, sake, vinegar, mirin and brown sugar and bring to the boil.

When the seasonings start boiling, add the chicken drumsticks to the saucepan, then cover with the drop-lid. Turn the heat down to medium and simmer for 40 minutes. Turn the drumsticks over a few times using tongs and baste them with the seasonings as they cook.

Meanwhile, place the eggs in a small saucepan, then cover with cold water and bring to the boil. Once just boiling, reduce the heat to medium-low and stir gently to turn the eggs (this should centre the yolks). Cook for 4 minutes uncovered.

Turn the heat off and let the eggs cook in the residual heat for 8 minutes with the lid on.

Drain, then submerge the eggs in cold water for 2 minutes to stop the cooking process. Peel the eggs when cool enough to handle.

When the 40 minutes cooking time for the chicken stew is up, add the peeled eggs and simmer, covered with the drop lid, for a final 10 minutes. Baste the chicken and eggs with the seasonings again as they cook.

Remove the stew from the heat and rest with the lid on for 20 minutes.

Cut the eggs in half to serve and serve the stew with plenty of rice on the side.

CHICKEN NANBAN
CHICKEN IN NANBAN SEASONINGS WITH TARTAR SAUCE

This is a typical dish from my home-town region of Kyushu and it's a real comfort food treat: fried chicken swiftly dipped in sweet vinegary sauce and topped with tartar sauce. Nanban is a classic example of what we call 'yoshoku' or Western-influenced cuisine. So much so that its meaning even translates as 'foreigner' in ancient Japanese. In this recipe, I marinate the meat in shio koji, which makes for an incredibly tender texture as the shio koji breaks down the protein and makes the meat extra juicy. However, if you can't find shio koji, regular sea salt works just as well.

4 boneless skin-on chicken thigh fillets
3 tbsp shio koji (or 2 pinches of sea salt)
50 g/generous ⅓ cup plain/all-purpose flour
1 egg, beaten
300 ml/1¼ cups vegetable oil
2 tbsp mirin
2 tbsp soy sauce
2 tbsp rice vinegar
leafy salad, to serve
lemon wedges, to serve

TARTAR SAUCE
2 UK large/US extra-large eggs, hard-boiled, cooled, peeled and finely chopped
2 tbsp finely chopped shallots
2 tbsp finely chopped gherkins
2 tbsp freshly chopped parsley
4 tbsp Japanese mayonnaise
2 tsp freshly squeezed lemon juice
salt, to taste

SERVES 4

Score the chicken flesh at intervals and place in a large dish. Sprinkle the flesh with the shio koji. Cover with clingfilm/plastic wrap or place in a resealable plastic bag (squeezing any air from the bag). Refrigerate and leave to marinate for at least 20 minutes and up to 2 hours. If using salt rather than shio koji, simply season and skip the marinating step and continue with the recipe.

Meanwhile, for the tartar sauce, mix together the finely chopped boiled eggs, shallots, gherkins and parsley in a small bowl. Mix in the mayonnaise, lemon juice and some salt to season. Refrigerate until needed.

Wipe off the shio koji (if using) and any moisture from the chicken with a paper towel. Lay out a dish containing the flour and another dish containing the egg. Roll the chicken thighs in the flour to give a light dusting, then dip into the beaten egg to coat all over.

Put the oil in a medium frying pan/skillet and heat to 180°C (350°F) over a high heat. To check that the oil is ready, drop a little egg into the oil. If it sizzles gently, the oil is ready. Reduce the heat to medium to maintain the temperature. Shallow-fry the chicken, two thighs at a time, for 5 minutes or until cooked through (depending on the thickness), turning over a few times until brown. Remove with a slotted spoon and transfer to a cooling rack. Repeat for the remaining chicken.

Heat the mirin, soy sauce and rice vinegar in a small saucepan over a low heat. Holding a cooked chicken thigh in tongs, briefly dip into the saucepan to season, then drain on a cooling rack. It will absorb the sauce instantly. Repeat for the remaining chicken.

To serve, cut the chicken widthways into 2-cm/¾-inch thick strips. Place each sliced thigh on a serving plate and pour some tartar sauce on top. Serve with a leafy salad and a lemon wedge for squeezing over.

MIZUTAKI NABE
CHICKEN HOT POT WITH PONZU DIPPING SAUCE

Mizutaki nabe is a type of nabe (hot pot) dish, where a selection of meat and vegetables are simmered together in a large pot. It is usually cooked and served right on the table (though you can also cook it on the hob/stovetop) and it is the perfect cosy dish to enjoy when the weather is cold. There are many types of nabes in Japan, however, I selected this particular one because it's a typical dish from Kyushu in southern Japan where I am from, and it reminds me of evenings spent with my family.

CHICKEN STOCK
2 chicken carcasses
30 g/1 oz. fresh ginger, unpeeled and thinly sliced
2 leeks, green parts only

CHICKEN MEATBALLS
400 g/14 oz. skinless boneless chicken thigh fillets
1 tsp sea salt
¼ tsp freshly ground black pepper
2 tsp peeled and grated fresh ginger
1 egg
1 tbsp katakuriko (potato starch) or cornflour/cornstarch
10 g/¼ cup finely chopped fresh chives

HOT POT
½ Chinese cabbage, roughly chopped
2 leeks, cut into 2-cm/¾-inch diagonal slices
4 fresh shiitake mushrooms
1 carrot, peeled and cut into 1-cm/½-inch thick pieces
40 g/1 cup spinach, blanched and very well drained
350 g/12 oz. firm tofu, diced into bite-sized pieces
yuzu kosho chilli/chili paste, to serve

PONZU DIPPING SAUCE
60 ml/¼ cup soy sauce
60 ml/¼ cup mirin
60 ml/¼ cup rice vinegar
2 tbsp freshly squeezed lime juice
10 cm/4 inches daikon radish, peeled, grated and excess water drained

hot plate, for serving at the table (optional)

SERVES 4

For the chicken stock, add the chicken carcasses, ginger and leek greens to a very large saucepan. Cover with water, then bring to the boil. Reduce the heat to low and simmer, uncovered, for at least 1 hour and up to 2 hours. Skim any scum off the surface and top up with water to make sure the bones stay covered.

Strain the stock and set aside (discarding the veg and carcasses). It should make about 1.5 litres/quarts.

Meanwhile, for the ponzu dipping sauce, mix together the soy sauce, mirin, rice vinegar and lime juice in a small bowl. Set aside.

To make the chicken meatballs, pulse the chicken in a food processor until minced/ground (not smooth) or finely chop with a knife. Mix the minced/ground chicken with the rest of the ingredients in a bowl.

(From this point, you can either cook the hot pot on the hob/stove, or if you have a hot plate, cook the hot pot on the table in the traditional Japanese way.)

For the hot pot, bring the stock to the boil in a large saucepan. Use two spoons to scoop out the chicken and make into oval-shaped meatballs. Add half of these to the stock along with half of all the vegetables and tofu*. Lower the heat and simmer for 7 minutes, until the meat and vegetables are cooked.

Divide the hot pot ingredients into serving bowls, leaving some stock in the cooking pot. Put the grated daikon into the ponzu dipping sauce and serve alongside the yuzu kosho chilli/chili paste.

Add the remaining vegetables, tofu and meatballs to the leftover stock in the pan and repeat the cooking process again while you eat the first batch of hot pot!

*Alternatively, you can cook all the meatballs, vegetables and tofu in one go if your saucepan is big enough.

YUDOFU
HOT WATER TOFU

The humble yet delicious yudofu is a tofu hot pot with a delicious, clean flavour. It might be made with few simple ingredients, but you'll understand why it is so loved by the people of Kyoto after trying it. This dish was originally eaten by Buddhist monks who were not allowed to eat meat or fish, and so appreciated tofu as an excellent source of protein. The warmth of the kombu broth, the slight sweetness of the tofu, its silky texture and the savouriness of the daikon and spring onion/scallion, makes this the perfect meal on a cold, wintry day.

650 g/1 lb. 7 oz. firm tofu, drained
1 litre/quart Kombu Dashi (see page 23)
Tsuyu Sauce (see page 74), to serve

TOPPINGS (OPTIONAL)
100 g/3½ oz. daikon radish, grated
2 spring onions/scallions, sliced
2 tbsp toasted white sesame seeds, ground
20 g/¾ oz. fresh ginger, peeled and grated
1 tablespoon katsuobushi (bonito flakes)
1 tsp yuzu kosho chilli/chili paste

SERVES 4

Cut the tofu into 4–6 large cubes.

Put the tofu into a medium-sized saucepan, then pour in the kombu dashi. The tofu should be completely immersed. Place the pan over a gentle low–medium heat and let it warm up slowly for 5 minutes or so. Think of the cooking process as giving the tofu a warm bath. Do not let it boil – if you overheat the tofu, it will become hard and small bubbles will appear on the surface.

To serve, dilute the tsuyu sauce with an equal amount of hot water (it's nice to use the cooked kombu dashi from the hot pot) and divide it between small individual serving bowls. With a slotted spoon, take the tofu out of its bath, and divide between the serving bowls.

Let your guests add some toppings of their choice for added texture and flavour.

SHABU SHABU
PORK & VEGETABLE HOT POT

This dish is one of the most famous hot pots. Shabu shabu ingredients are served raw and cooked at the table during the meal, similar to fondue, so you will need a hot plate for this recipe. Give your guests individual serving bowls and plenty of sesame dipping sauce. The meal is enjoyed in three stages: the meat, followed by the tofu, noodles and vegetables and finished with rice and egg cooked in the flavour-packed broth to make a 'porridge', if you still have room! The meat for this recipe needs to be as thinly sliced as Parma ham/Prosciutto, which is very difficult to do at home, so it is best to buy it ready-sliced from a Japanese supermarket or grocery store.

350 g/12 oz. firm tofu

100 g/3½ oz. dried harusame noodles

300 g/10½ oz. ready-cut thinly sliced pork loin from a Japanese supermarket/grocery store

½ Chinese cabbage, cut into 5-cm/2-inch length strips

2 leeks, thinly sliced diagonally

1 carrot, peeled and shaved into ribbons

200 g/7 oz. fresh enoki mushrooms or any other mushrooms

40 g/1½ oz. wild rocket/arugula

Ponzu Dipping Sauce (see page 128), to serve

SOUP BASE

1 litre/quart Kombu Dashi (see page 23)

SESAME DIPPING SAUCE

3 tbsp Japanese sesame paste (or light tahini)

1 tbsp white miso

1½ tbsp rice vinegar

3 tbsp mirin

3½ tbsp light soy sauce

1 tsp agave syrup

½ tbsp sesame oil

1 garlic clove, grated

50 ml/3½ tbsp Kombu Dashi (see page 23)

PORRIDGE (OPTIONAL)

200 g/1½ cups cooked Japanese rice

1 egg, beaten

sea salt and freshly ground black pepper

hot plate, for serving at the table

SERVES 4

Drain and dice the tofu into eight cubes.

Cook the harusame noodles in a pan of boiling water for about 2 minutes until soft, then drain. Rinse under cold water to stop the noodles from sticking to each other. (They become hard once cold, but you will cook them again in the hot pot.) Set aside.

For the dipping sauce, mix the sesame paste and miso with the vinegar until smooth, then mix in the rest of the ingredients slowly. Take care because the sesame paste may separate if liquid is added quickly.

Place all the meat, tofu and vegetables out on a large serving plate.

Bring the kombu dashi to the boil in a large saucepan on the hot plate at your dining table.

Ask your guests to dip the thinly sliced meat in the simmering dashi using a pair of cooking chopsticks (don't eat the meat after using cooking chopsticks, you can use your eating chopsticks for this). The thinly sliced pork should turn white and be cooked through within about 10 seconds. Dip into the sesame dipping sauce or ponzu dipping sauce to eat.

Add some of the vegetables, noodles and tofu to the stock in the pot and bring it to the boil again. Then lower the heat and simmer for 4 minutes. When the vegetables are cooked, enjoy with the sesame dipping sauce, and then add more to the pot as needed.

Finally, add the rice to the remaining stock and simmer for 10 minutes over a low heat. Pour the beaten egg over and stir in to make the 'porridge'. Season with salt and pepper and serve.

SUKIYAKI NABE
BEEF HOT POT

Before sushi became a global phenomenon, Japan's most famous culinary export was sukiyaki. A hot pot of thinly sliced beef and vegetables served in a sauce of dashi, tamari and other seasonings. Sukiyaki even had its own hit song in 1961 when Japanese crooner Kyu Sakamoto's 'sukiyaki' song reached number one in the US, Canada, Norway and Japan. The lyrics had nothing to do with the dish, but it certainly helped put it on the map!

350 g/12 oz. firm tofu
500 g/1 lb. 2 oz. frozen udon
  noodles
8 fresh shiitake mushrooms
80 g/3 oz. fresh enoki
  mushrooms
2 tbsp vegetable oil
500 g/1 lb. 2 oz. ready-cut
  thinly sliced sirloin or rib
  eye of beef from a Japanese
  supermarket/grocery store
½ Chinese cabbage, cut into
  5-cm/2-inch length strips
2 leeks, thinly sliced
  diagonally
40 g/1½ oz. watercress
4 organic eggs, to serve

SUKIYAKI SAUCE
100 ml/⅓ cup plus 1 tbsp
  tamari (or soy sauce)
50 ml/3½ tbsp sake
50 ml/3½ tbsp mirin
2 tbsp soft light brown sugar
250 ml/1 cup plus 1 tbsp
  Kombu Dashi (see page 23)

*hot plate, for serving at the
  table (optional)*

SERVES 4

Drain and dice the tofu into eight cubes.

Defrost the udon noodles by immersing them in just-boiled water. Drain well and set aside.

Remove and discard the stems of the shiitake mushrooms. Trim the bottom off the enoki mushrooms, then tear into small bunches. Set both mushrooms aside.

To make the sukiyaki sauce, combine the tamari (or soy sauce), sake, mirin, brown sugar and kombu dashi. Stir until the sugar has dissolved. Set aside.

Add 1 tablespoon of the vegetable oil to a frying pan/skillet over a high heat. Add the beef and fry for about 1 minute until the outside is just browned. Do not cook the meat through, you want the inside to be medium-rare. Set aside, then repeat for the remaining beef and set aside.

From this point, you can either cook the hot pot on the hob/stove, or if you have a hot plate, cook the hot pot on the table in the traditional Japanese way. Add the sukiyaki sauce to a large saucepan and bring to the boil.

Add the seared beef, prepared tofu and mushrooms and the Chinese cabbage, leeks and noodles. Cover with a lid and bring to the boil again, then reduce the heat to low and simmer for 4 minutes until the cabbage is cooked. Add the watercress, cover and cook for 1 minute more.

To serve, break the eggs into small individual bowls and beat gently. Divide the sukiyaki nabe into serving bowls (or let everyone help themselves if cooking the dish at the table). Let each guest dip the cooked ingredients from their hot pot into the raw egg and enjoy warm.

BUTA NO KAKUNI
BRAISED CUBES OF PORK BELLY

Buta no kakuni is a braised pork dish which literally means 'square-simmered pork'. Although most probably originating from China, it has become a regional speciality of southern Kyushu. As Nagasaki was an important trading port from the 16th century until the Meiji era, many varieties of food there were influenced by the mixing of cultures from that period. To keep the cubic shapes of pork intact while cooking, choose a thick piece of pork belly with at least three layers of alternating lean meat and fat. This gives a melt-in-the-mouth effect and a beautiful presentation.

1.2 kg/2⅔ lb. boneless pork belly, skin on
1 tbsp vegetable oil
30 g/1 oz. fresh ginger, unpeeled, thinly sliced
10 cm/4 inches leek, green part only
2 turnips, halved (or ⅓ length of daikon white radish, peeled and cut into 3-cm/1¼-inch round slices)
50 ml/3½ tbsp sake
50 ml/3½ tbsp mirin
100 ml/⅓ cup plus 1 tbsp soy sauce
5 tbsp soft light brown sugar
3 tbsp tamari
10 x 10-cm/4 x 4-inch piece of kombu

TO SERVE
English mustard
1 spring onion/scallion, finely shredded

medium-sized pressure cooker (optional)

SERVES 4

Cut the pork belly into 6 x 18-cm/2½ x 7-inch pieces, or so that it will fit inside your cooker or saucepan. Rub the vegetable oil all over the surface of the pork.

Heat a large frying pan/skillet over a high heat. Sear the pork, skin-side down for 1 minute, then turn to brown all the other sides for a couple of minutes.

Remove the pork and wipe off excess oil with a paper towel. Add 1 litre/quart of water, the ginger, leek and the pork to the pressure cooker or a large, heavy-based saucepan. Place the lid on and bring to the boil.

Once pressure has been reached or the liquid is boiling, turn the heat down to low and simmer for 30 minutes if using a pressure cooker or 1½ hours if cooking in a regular saucepan (a pressure cooker is much faster!).

Remove the pressure cooker or saucepan from the heat (wait for the pressure to naturally release if using a pressure cooker), then take the pork out and drain the water, discarding the liquid, leek and ginger. Let the pork cool for 10 minutes, then cut it into eight large cubes.

Meanwhile, boil the turnips for 5 minutes (or the daikon radish for 10 minutes) until tender. Drain well.

Add the sake, mirin, soy sauce, brown sugar, tamari, kombu, pork, turnips or daikon radish and 800 ml/3⅓ cups water back into the pressure cooker or large saucepan. Place the lid on, then bring to the boil.

Once pressure has been reached or the liquid is boiling, turn the heat to low and simmer for 45 minutes if using a pressure cooker or 2 hours if using a saucepan.

Turn off the heat, (let the pressure naturally release if using a pressure cooker), and let the pork rest for 20 minutes before serving with English mustard. Garnish with shredded spring onion/scallion.

TUNA NO TATAKI
SEARED TUNA WITH PONZU JELLY

This has become my signature dish and I always receive so many compliments each time I present it to guests or clients. Not only is it a stunning and stylish dish to serve, bursting with colours, but also a delight for the taste buds with tart ponzu jelly coating the mellow avocado and meaty tuna. Simple and elegant, it's heaven on a plate!

1 tbsp grated garlic

1 tbsp peeled and grated fresh ginger

2 tbsp vegetable oil

4 tuna steaks or 800 g/ 1¾ lb. tuna sliced into 2-cm/¾-inch thick steaks

a pinch of sea salt and freshly ground black pepper

PONZU JELLY

50 ml/3½ tbsp rice vinegar

50 ml/3½ tbsp light soy sauce

50 ml/3½ tbsp mirin

¼ tsp fine sea salt

1 tsp golden caster sugar

1½ tsp kanten (agar flakes), if you use kanten powder, then use ½ tsp

1 tbsp katakuriko (potato starch) or cornflour/ cornstarch, mixed with 1 tbsp of cold water

2 tbsp freshly squeezed lime juice

TO SERVE

2 ripe avocados, peeled, pitted and thinly sliced

salad leaves

2 red radishes, thinly sliced

1 shallot, finely chopped, soaked in water to remove bitterness and drained

2 tbsp deep-fried garlic chips

micro herbs

SERVES 4

To make the ponzu jelly, place the rice vinegar, light soy sauce, mirin, salt, sugar and kanten (agar flakes) in a medium saucepan with 150 ml/⅔ cup water. Stir while bringing to the boil over a medium heat, then lower the heat and simmer for 3–5 minutes until the kanten (agar flakes) have dissolved.

Pour the katakuriko (potato starch) or cornflour/ cornstarch mixture in slowly, and stir until the mixture has thickened. Finally, squeeze in the lime juice and mix in well.

Pour the ponzu jelly into a bowl, leave to cool and then refrigerate for 40–60 minutes until soft-set (it should still be just pourable).

Meanwhile, mix the grated garlic and ginger together with the oil and spread on each side of the tuna steaks, then season with the salt and pepper.

Heat a griddle pan/grill pan to hot, and sear the tuna for 45 seconds on each side for rare.

Let the tuna steaks cool, then refrigerate for 20 minutes. Slice the chilled tuna steaks widthways into 5-mm/¼-inch thick slices.

To serve, alternate slices of avocado with slices of a tuna steak, then pour some of the ponzu jelly over the top. Garnish with salad leaves and sliced radishes, finely chopped shallot, garlic chips and micro herbs.

NOTE This recipe is pescatarian, but if you are a meat eater, you can substitute the kanten (agar flakes) and the katakuriko (potato starch) for one sheet of gelatine for the ponzu jelly. However, if you use gelatine, the jelly will take around 3 hours longer to set.

TONYU NABE
SEAFOOD & SOY MILK HOT POT

If you like chowder, this hot pot is for you! It's a hearty fish soup that is most definitely still Japanese, with a base of seasoned dashi and soy milk. It is creamy but nutritious and actually quite low in fat. In Japanese cuisine, you will often find an abundance of different textures, just like in this dish, where you'll enjoy biting into the soft crumbly tofu, the chewy noodles and the spongy aburaage. A very Japanese chowder indeed!

350 g/12 oz. firm tofu
15 g/½ oz. aburaage (thinly sliced deep-fried tofu)
100 g/3½ oz. dried harusame noodles
400 g/14 oz. white fish such as sea bass, sea bream, haddock or monkfish, cut into bite-sized pieces
4 fresh king prawns/jumbo shrimp in shells
½ Chinese cabbage, cut into 5-cm/2-inch length strips
2 leeks, thinly sliced diagonally
1 carrot, peeled and shaved into ribbons
100 g/3½ oz. fresh shimeji mushrooms or any other mushrooms, stems removed
40 g/1½ oz. wild rocket/arugula
2 tsp grated garlic

SOUP BASE
1 litre/quart Kombu Dashi (see page 23)
500 ml/2 cups plus 2 tbsp soy milk
6 tbsp white miso
3 tbsp mirin

SERVES 4

Drain and dice the tofu into eight cubes and set aside.

Rinse the aburaage in just-boiled water, then wipe dry with a paper towel to remove excess oil on the surface. Cut the aburaage into medium-sized triangles. Set aside.

Cook the harusame noodles in a pan of boiling water for about 2 minutes until soft, then drain. Rinse under cold water to stop the noodles from sticking to each other. (They become hard once cold, but you will cook them again in the hot pot.) Set aside.

For the soup base, bring the kombu dashi to the boil in a large saucepan. Pour the soy milk into the boiling dashi, then turn the heat down to medium and bring to a simmer. Mix the white miso and mirin together in a cup, making sure the miso is well dissolved, and stir into the soy milk base.

Add the fish, prawns/shrimp, cabbage, leeks, carrot, mushrooms and rocket/arugula to the pan and simmer for about 7 minutes over a medium heat, uncovered, until the fish, seafood and vegetables are all cooked. Be careful not to let the hot pot boil again, or the soy milk will coagulate.

Finally, stir in the grated garlic, then remove from the heat and serve.

NOTE If all the ingredients do not fit in your pan at once, cook them in two or three batches in the soy milk broth. If cooking in batches, you can reasonably eat the first batch while the second is cooking!

SAKANA NO MUSHIMONO
STEAMED FISH 'PILLOWS' & CLAMS WITH YUZU PONZU

This is my go-to recipe for a simple yet delicious dinner party supper. Traditionally, Japanese households would use a steamer to cook these, as not all have ovens. But, Western kitchens being all perfectly equipped, I find oven-cooking works just as well! When heated up, these fish parcels swell up like pillows, hence their name. Don't forget to sprinkle sake on the fish, as this is what creates the steam inside the pillow and cooks the fish beautifully. Place the pillows on dinner plates and open them in front of your guests for maximum entertainment!

400 g/14 oz. fresh clams in shells

15 g/1 tbsp fine sea salt dissolved in 500 ml/2 cups plus 2 tbsp cold water (if using live clams)

4 x 100 g/3½ oz. fillets of sea bass or sea bream (skin-on)

2 tbsp shio koji (if available) or ½ tsp sea salt

2 leeks, sliced into 1-cm/ ½-inch round slices

100 g/3½ oz. broccoli florets, halved

4 tbsp sake

200 ml/generous ¾ cup Yuzu Ponzu (see page 169), to serve

4 x 50-cm/20-inch length pieces of extra-thick foil

SERVES 4

Scrub the clam shells to remove any dirt from the outside. Clams bought from the supermarket will already have been 'purged' – had the sand cleaned out of them. If you have bought wild clams from a fishmonger, spread them in a shallow flat container without overlapping. Pour over the salt water to just cover the heads of the clams. Cover with foil and refrigerate for 2 hours. The clams will spit out any sand inside. Rinse once more before using.

Sprinkle the fish fillets with the shio koji (if using) or the sea salt and place each one in a resealable plastic bag, squeezing out any air. Refrigerate and leave to marinate in the shio koji for 2 hours, or in the salt for 20 minutes.

Preheat the oven to 180°C (350°F) Gas 4.

Wipe off the shio koji or salt and any moisture from the fish with paper towels. Make a shallow cross-shaped cut in the skin on the centre of each fish fillet.

On one side (not in the middle) of each piece of foil, position a layer of leek slices (so the fish won't stick to the foil), then place the fish on top, skin-side up. Scatter the broccoli florets and clams around the fish. Sprinkle 1 tablespoon of sake over each fish fillet, then fold the empty half of the foil over the fish and fold the edges tightly together to seal, so that no steam can escape.

Place the fish pillows on the bottom rack of the preheated oven, making sure there is about 10 cm/ 4 inches of space above, as they will swell when cooking. Cook for 12 minutes, for medium-sized fish fillets.

Carefully remove the hot parcels from the oven and leave for 2 minutes. Place onto serving plates and cut open the parcels with a knife. Pour the yuzu ponzu over the fish and serve straight from the parcels.

CHAN CHAN YAKI
FRIED & STEAMED SALMON IN MISO GARLIC SAUCE

This native recipe from Hokkaido, Japan's most northern island, consists of pan-frying (yaki) salmon and some assorted vegetables, then steaming the lot in sake and serving it in miso sauce. It's uncertain where the 'chan chan' part of the name comes from, but one story says it is simply the sound of the ingredients frying! I like to add a little garlic to the miso sauce for an extra burst of flavour.

1 tbsp vegetable oil
2 skin-on salmon fillets
¼ Savoy cabbage, diced into
    bite-sized pieces
1 medium onion, thinly sliced
½ carrot, peeled and cut into
    matchsticks
60 g/2¼ oz. fresh shimeji
    mushrooms, bottoms
    trimmed and separated
2 tbsp sake
1 tbsp butter, to serve

MISO GARLIC SAUCE
2 garlic cloves, grated
3 tbsp red miso
2 tbsp mirin

*large frying pan/skillet
    with a lid*

SERVES 2

For the miso garlic sauce, in a small bowl, combine the grated garlic with the red miso and mirin, then stir until combined. Set aside.

Heat the vegetable oil in the large frying pan/skillet over a high heat. Fry both the salmon fillets, skin-side down for 2–3 minutes, or until the skin has browned.

Flip over and fry for 2 more minutes, then remove the salmon from the pan and set aside.

Add all the vegetables and mushrooms to the hot pan and stir-fry for 2 minutes.

Put the salmon fillets back into the pan, nestled among the vegetables, and pour in the sake around the salmon. Place a lid over the frying pan/skillet and let the fish steam over a medium heat for 1 minute to cook off the alcohol.

Add the miso garlic sauce to the pan and stir gently to evenly coat the ingredients. Put the lid back on and simmer for 4–5 minutes over a medium-high heat until the salmon is perfectly cooked all the way through.

When ready to serve, top each salmon fillet with a sliver of butter and allow it to melt a little. Serve hot.

SAKANA NO NITSUKE
SOY-SIMMERED LEMON SOLE

*When my mum makes this dish, my dad is always very happy and eats it with 'atsukan'
hot sake. Japan is known outside of its shores for its grilled or raw fish dishes, but
simmered fish recipes are real home-cooking staples, and I ate them regularly at
home when I was growing up. This is still one of my favourite ways of eating fish.
The secret is to boil the seasonings first, then add the fish so as not to lose any of
the flavours. This recipe also works well with other types of fish like sea bream, sea
bass and dover sole.*

650 g/1 lb. 7 oz. whole lemon
   sole fillet, skin-on and
   bone-in
½ tsp fine sea salt
½ daikon white radish, peeled
   and cut into 3-cm/1¼-inch
   rounds
100 ml/⅓ cup plus 1 tbsp sake
3 tbsp soy sauce
1 tbsp mirin
1½ tbsp soft light brown sugar
20 g/¾ oz. fresh ginger,
   peeled and thinly sliced
1 garlic clove, crushed
1 spring onion/scallion,
   finely shredded, to garnish
cooked rice of your choice
   (see page 29), to serve

*large, shallow saucepan or
   deep frying pan/skillet with
   a drop-lid or a homemade
   drop-lid (see page 19)*

SERVES 4

Scrape the skin of the fish fillet from the tail end to the
head end, using the back of a knife to remove the scales.

Cut the lemon sole into four pieces widthways across
the spine. Score a cross pattern into the skin of the fish.

Sprinkle the salt on the flesh of the fish, cover with
clingfilm/plastic wrap and refrigerate for 20 minutes.

Meanwhile, cook the daikon in a small pan of boiling
water for 10 minutes, then drain well. Set aside.

In the separate large, shallow saucepan or the deep
frying pan/skillet, combine the sake, soy sauce, mirin,
brown sugar, ginger and garlic with 100 ml/⅓ cup plus
1 tbsp water. Bring to the boil.

Place the fish in the saucepan with the seasonings
and bring to the boil again. Reduce the heat and bring
the contents of the pan to a simmer, basting the fish with
the simmering liquid.

Place a drop-lid on top of the fish and turn the heat
to its lowest setting. Simmer gently for 10 minutes or until
the fish is cooked through. Add the daikon slices for the
last 3 minutes of the cooking time to absorb the flavours.

When the fish is cooked, remove it from the heat.
Serve the simmered fish with plenty of the cooking liquid,
some pieces of daikon and rice on the side. Garnish with
shredded spring onion/scallion.

SABA NO MISONI
MISO-SIMMERED MACKEREL

Mackerel is a delicious fish, inexpensive and particularly good for you thanks to its richness in omega 3. It can be enjoyed all year round, although it is at its very best in September and October, when its fatty body is at its plumpest. Mackerel is a very common fish in Japan, enjoyed in many different ways: grilled, stewed, fried or marinated in vinegar. To check for its freshness: look for clear eyes, a bright blue back and red gills. Fresh mackerel has flesh which offers elasticity to the touch and its skin should be glossy and taut. Mackerel deteriorates quickly in quality so try and purchase the freshest fillets you can buy.

4 mackerel fillets, skin-on
2 tbsp soy sauce
2 tbsp sake
1 tbsp soft light brown sugar
20 g/¾ oz. fresh ginger, peeled and thinly sliced
1 tbsp vegetable oil
1 leek, sliced into 3-cm/1¼-inch length pieces
2 tbsp red miso
2 tbsp mirin
cooked rice of your choice (see page 29), to serve

large, shallow saucepan or deep frying pan/skillet with a drop-lid or a homemade drop-lid (see page 19)

SERVES 4

Cut each mackerel fillet in half widthways. Score a cross onto the skin of each using a sharp knife.

In the large, shallow saucepan or deep frying pan/skillet, combine 300 ml/1¼ cups water with the soy sauce, sake, brown sugar and ginger. Bring to the boil.

Put the mackerel, skin-side up, into the boiling seasonings in the pan. Baste the skin of the mackerel with the seasonings, then cover the pan with the drop-lid. Reduce the heat to low and simmer gently for 7 minutes.

Meanwhile, heat the vegetable oil in a frying pan/skillet over a medium-high heat and fry the leek slices for 2 minutes just until browned, then add them to the mackerel in the pan.

Mix the miso and mirin together in a cup to form a loose paste and pour over the mackerel in the pan.

Simmer for 5 minutes more, covered with the drop-lid, until the cooking liquid has thickened into a sauce. Turn the heat off and leave to cool for 20 minutes in the pan.

Serve the mackerel and leeks with the thinly sliced simmered fresh ginger for an extra punch of flavour, and some fluffy cooked rice on the side.

YAKI TOFU
TOFU STEAKS WITH SESAME & SOY DRESSING

This recipe for a delicious yet simple meatless supper has substantial texture and satisfying flavour. Tofu is a staple of Japanese cuisine, eaten by millions every day. It comes in several different firmnesses, making it a super versatile ingredient to cook with. All options are made from the same simple ingredients: soy beans, nigari (a coagulant) and 90% water. It is a great source of protein and calcium and is low in calories. This sesame and soy dressing adds umami richness to the dish.

800 g/1¾ lb. firm tofu, drained
80 g/2¾ oz. shio koji (or 1 tsp sea salt)
50 g/1¾ oz. katakuriko (potato starch) or cornflour/cornstarch
2 tbsp vegetable oil

SESAME & SOY DRESSING
2 tbsp toasted sesame oil
2 tbsp vegetable oil
2 tbsp flaked/slivered almonds
2 garlic cloves, thinly sliced
20 g/¾ oz. fresh ginger, peeled and finely chopped
2 spring onions/scallions, thinly sliced
3 tbsp soy sauce
2 tbsp mirin
2 tbsp toasted white sesame seeds
1 tbsp dried goji berries
sea salt
2 red radishes, cut into matchsticks, to serve
mixed leaf salad, to serve

SERVES 4

If you are using shio koji, slice the tofu into four 'steaks'. Rub the surface of the tofu with the shio koji and place in a resealable plastic bag, squeezing out any air. Refrigerate and leave to marinate for a minimum of 20 minutes or overnight. The shio koji will draw out excess moisture.

If you are using sea salt instead of shio koji, wrap the tofu in plenty of paper towels and compress under a heavy kitchen utensil for 30 minutes to remove excess water. Slice the tofu into four 'steaks'. Rub the surface of the tofu with the salt to season and skip the marinating step.

To make the sesame and soy dressing, combine the toasted sesame oil and vegetable oil in a saucepan over a medium heat. When it becomes hot (but not smoking), fry the almonds and garlic, stirring regularly, until pale golden in colour. Take care that they don't burn.

Turn the heat off and transfer the almonds and garlic to a paper towel to drain off any excess oil.

Add the ginger and spring onions/scallions to the oil in the pan while it is still hot and let them sizzle in the residual heat as the oil cools.

Once the oil has cooled down, stir in the soy sauce, mirin, toasted sesame seeds and goji berries. Season the oil with a little sea salt.

Wipe the tofu 'steaks' with paper towels (if needed) to remove any excess moisture or shio koji. Lightly coat the tofu 'steaks' in the katakuriko (potato starch) or cornflour/cornstarch. Place the vegetable oil in a frying pan/skillet over a medium heat and fry the tofu slices for 1–2 minutes on each side until crisp.

Pour the sesame and soy dressing over the tofu 'steaks' to serve and garnish with the fried almonds and garlic and sliced radishes. Serve with mixed leaf salad.

SIDES &
DRESSINGS

HIJIKI NO NIMONO
SIMMERED HIJIKI SEAWEED & VEGETABLES

You have probably noticed by now that we Japanese eat a lot of seaweed... the reason for this is that Japanese soil lacks the calcium that luckily fresh and preserved seaweed is rich in. We say in Japan that eating hijiki every day will make your hair strong, thick and lustrous – so why not try it for yourself? Brown and twig-looking, this seaweed almost tastes of the forest and goes perfectly in this umami-rich salad. Konnyaku adds a unique meaty texture and volume to this dish, but if you cannot find this, then just substitute with extra vegetables for more texture.

12 g/¼–½ oz. dried hijiki seaweed
1 piece of aburaage (thinly sliced deep-fried tofu)
100 g/3½ oz. konnyaku block
2 tbsp toasted sesame oil
1 carrot, peeled and cut into matchsticks
1 celery stick, thinly sliced diagonally
1 garlic clove, thinly sliced
30 g/1 oz. fresh or defrosted frozen garden peas
3 tbsp soy sauce
3 tbsp mirin
2 tbsp balsamic vinegar
sea salt

OPTIONAL GARNISHES
1 tsp toasted sesame seeds
1 tbsp toasted crushed almonds
½ tsp toasted coriander seeds
½ tsp pink peppercorns

SERVES 4 AS A SIDE

Soak the hijiki in cold water for 15 minutes to reconstitute, then drain.

Rinse the aburaage in just-boiled water, then wipe dry with a paper towel to remove excess oil on the surface. Slice the aburaage into strips. Set aside.

Boil the konnyaku in a pan of salted water for 3 minutes to remove any smell, then cut it into 3-cm/1¼-inch length skinny sticks.

Heat a frying pan/skillet over a high heat, and add the sesame oil. Fry the hijiki seaweed, aburaage, konnyaku, carrot, celery and garlic for 3–4 minutes, stirring.

Add the garden peas to the pan. Combine the soy sauce, mirin and balsamic vinegar in a small bowl, then pour over the hijiki mixture in the pan. Turn the heat down to medium and simmer for 3 minutes until the seasonings have evaporated.

Remove to a serving bowl and leave the salad to cool to room temperature before serving.

Garnish the salad with toasted sesame seeds or some toasted crushed almonds, toasted coriander seeds or pink peppercorns for different plays on flavours and textures. Try anything you have in your store cupboard!

Leftovers will keep for a few days in the fridge, and go perfectly well in a bento box for lunch!

KIMPIRA
SPICY LOTUS ROOT SALAD

Kimpira is one of those dishes that may sound curious to Western palates, but is hugely popular all over Japan. A crunchy salad of quickly stir-fried and then simmered root vegetables in a sweet soy sauce with a hint of toasted sesame flavour. Once you've tried it, you will understand instantly why it's such a hit in Japan. Serve with a glass of sake for real authenticity!

1 aburaage (thinly sliced deep-fried tofu)

1 tbsp toasted sesame oil

300 g/10½ oz. fresh renkon (lotus root), peeled and thinly sliced into rounds (frozen sliced renkon is also available)

1 carrot, peeled and sliced into thin strips

2 tsp soft light brown sugar

2 tbsp mirin

3 tbsp soy sauce

1 dried red chilli/chili, deseeded and thinly sliced

1 tbsp ground toasted white sesame seeds, to serve

a pinch of dried red chilli/chili shreds, to serve (optional)

large frying pan/skillet with a lid

SERVES 4 AS A SIDE

Rinse the aburaage in just-boiled water, then wipe dry with a paper towel to remove excess oil on the surface. Dice the aburaage.

Heat a large frying pan/skillet over a medium heat. Add the toasted sesame oil and let it warm through.

Add the renkon (lotus root) and carrot and fry for 2 minutes, stirring to let the oil coat all the vegetables.

Add the brown sugar, mirin and 2 tablespoons of the soy sauce. Sprinkle over the sliced chilli/chile and stir in.

Add 75 ml/⅓ cup of water to the pan and bring to the boil. Cover the pan with a lid, reduce the heat to medium and simmer for 4 minutes until the renkon (lotus root) is tender.

Add the remaining 1 tablespoon of soy sauce, then increase the heat and simmer rapidly for 1–2 minutes until the liquid has evaporated and the vegetables have become nicely caramelized.

Serve the warm salad sprinkled with the ground toasted sesame seeds to give some aroma. Add dried red chilli/chili shreds if you like it hot.

VARIATIONS
You can use other types of root vegetables in place of the renkon (lotus root) in this recipe. Try parsnips, potatoes and even celery to give a crisp texture. It is very important not to overcook the vegetables for this salad, as you don't want them to lose their texture.

WAKAME TO KYURI NO AEMONO
WAKAME & CUCUMBER SALAD WITH SESAME DRESSING

This is a variation on the well-known sunomono, or sweet vinegared cucumber and wakame salad. Thin slices of cucumber and wakame seaweed in a slightly sweet, slightly sharp sesame dressing. This refreshing side dish is very easy to make and the creamy sesame dressing makes it incredibly moreish, but it's so low in calories that you can happily enjoy seconds or even thirds!

4 tbsp dried wakame seaweed
1 cucumber, very thinly sliced
½ tsp fine sea salt
2 tsp ground toasted white
  sesame seeds, to garnish

SESAME DRESSING
2 tbsp Japanese sesame paste
  (or light tahini)
2 tbsp rice vinegar
2 tbsp mirin
1½ tbsp light soy sauce
2 tsp clear honey

SERVES 4 AS A SIDE

In a bowl, reconstitute the dried wakame in 1 litre/quart of cold water for 5 minutes, then drain well.

Place the cucumber slices in a bowl and sprinkle with the salt. Stir so that the salt comes into contact with all the surfaces of the cucumber. Rub the cucumber lightly and leave for 10 minutes at room temperature. This will help remove any excess water and keep it crisp.

After 10 minutes, rinse and squeeze out any excess water from the cucumber slices and then toss together with the wakame in a bowl to combine.

To make the sesame dressing, mix the Japanese sesame paste (or light tahini) and rice vinegar together in a bowl to a smooth consistency. Add the mirin, light soy sauce and honey all slowly one spoonful at a time, mixing between each addition, until smooth and well combined. Don't add the ingredients too quickly or the sesame paste may separate.

When you are ready to serve, dress the cucumber and wakame with the sesame dressing and garnish the salad with the ground toasted white sesame seeds.

POTATO SALADA
JAPANESE-STYLE POTATO SALAD

This salad is a staple of Japanese home cooking: it's easy to make and you probably have most of the ingredients in your store cupboard already. But what makes this salad inherently Japanese, then? Firstly, the use of the Japanese mayonnaise, which is slightly more vinegary and sweet than European mayonnaise. Also, the dense and starchy 'hoku hoku' texture of the hand-crushed potatoes and the fresh crunch you get from the cucumber and onion.

250 g/9 oz. waxy potatoes (such as Charlotte potatoes)
250 g/9 oz. new potatoes
¼ onion, sliced along the grain
⅓ cucumber, thinly sliced
⅓ tsp fine sea salt
60 g/¼ cup Japanese Kewpie mayonnaise
½ tbsp rice vinegar
½ tbsp wholegrain mustard
20 g/¾ oz. Cheddar cheese, grated
a pinch of salt
a pinch of ground white pepper
50 g/1¾ oz. cured ham, diced into small cubes

TO GARNISH
1 hard-boiled egg, cooled and peeled
2 sprigs parsley, freshly chopped

SERVES 4 AS A SIDE

Combine the waxy potatoes and new potatoes in a medium saucepan and cover with water. Add the lid to the pan and bring to the boil.

Reduce the heat to medium-high and simmer for 15 minutes until the potatoes are cooked. Drain well and leave in a colander until completely dry and still warm but cool enough to handle.

Meanwhile, soak the sliced onion in water for 10 minutes to remove any bitter taste. Drain and set aside.

Place the cucumber slices in a bowl and sprinkle with the fine sea salt. Stir so that the salt comes into contact with all the surfaces of the cucumber. Rub the cucumber lightly and leave for 10 minutes at room temperature. This will help remove any excess water and keep it crisp.

Rinse and squeeze out any excess water from the cucumber slices and set aside.

In a large bowl, mix together the Japanese mayonnaise, rice vinegar, wholegrain mustard, grated cheese, salt and pepper.

Peel the skins off the boiled potatoes while they are still warm and discard. Crush the potatoes by hand to a semi-mashed consistency, leaving some bigger and some smaller pieces for interesting texture. Add the crushed potatoes to the bowl with the mayonnaise mixture. Add the diced ham, cucumber and onion and mix everything together well.

To garnish, grate the hard-boiled egg over the potato salad and sprinkle with the chopped parsley. Refrigerate until ready to serve.

NOTE This dish is perfect for making a day in advance, as the flavours improve even more and the texture becomes slightly smoother as the cucumber and onion draw out some water.

TOMATO NO OHITASHI
TOMATOES MARINATED IN DASHI JELLY

This wonderfully light and refreshing dish is the perfect recipe to cool you down on a hot summers day. Ohitashi is the method of steeping the tomatoes (or any other vegetable) in dashi stock. Beforehand, the tomatoes are blanched and shocked (plunged into ice-cold water to stop the cooking process), leaving them partially cooked. This means the tomatoes keep their structure but can now also absorb the umami-rich flavours of the dashi seasonings.

6 large tomatoes
1 gelatine sheet
200 ml/generous ¾ cup Kombu & Katsuobushi Dashi (see page 24)
2 tbsp light soy sauce
2 tbsp mirin

MAKES 6

Bring 1 litre/quart of water to the boil in a large saucepan.

Make a shallow cut anywhere on the skin of each tomato using the tip of a sharp knife (just to break the skin). Place all the tomatoes in a metal sieve/strainer and lower into the boiling water for 20 seconds.

When you see the skins begin to peel, quickly remove the sieve/strainer with the tomatoes and plunge into a bowl of iced water to stop the cooking process. Leave the tomatoes to cool in the iced water and then remove and discard the skins. Leave the leaves on for decoration, if you like – it also makes them easier to handle.

Leave the gelatine to soak in a cup of cold water for 10 minutes.

Meanwhile, combine the dashi, light soy sauce and mirin in a small saucepan and bring to the boil.

Turn off the heat and leave to cool for 20 minutes.

Once it has softened, remove the gelatine from the water, gently squeeze out any excess water and add to the dashi mixture while it is still warm. Stir in until dissolved.

Place the skinned tomatoes into a large resealable plastic bag (or use two smaller bags). Add the cooled dashi jelly mixture and make sure that the tomatoes are immersed in the seasonings. Dip the bag in a bowl of cold water to remove any air and seal immediately so it is almost vacuum-packed. Leave to marinate in the fridge for at least 4 hours until the jelly is softly set. (The marinated tomatoes will become even more flavoursome if marinated for longer – you can leave them for up to 2 days.)

Cut each tomato into eight wedges and serve with some of the dashi jelly.

ASA ZUKE
QUICK PICKLED VEGETABLES

In Japan, we've been enjoying pickles for hundreds of years. Before fridges or freezers existed, it was our way of preserving fresh vegetables and enjoying them throughout the year. Pickles (or tsukemono) have become part of our daily diet, and there are many types. Takuan (pickled daikon) or gari (pickled ginger) normally take from a week up to several months to make. This asa zuke ('lightly pickled') recipe will help you make tasty pickles in no time!

300 g/10½ oz. mixture of fresh vegetables
   (such as carrots, cucumber, radishes
   and/or Chinese cabbage)
1 tsp sea salt
1 tsp kombu stock powder
1 tsp golden caster sugar
1 tsp grated yuzu zest (or a mixture of
   grated orange and lime zest instead)
a pinch of shichimi (Japanese spice mix)

SERVES 4 AS A SIDE

Peel (as appropriate) and thinly slice all the vegetables. Chop any larger slices into bite-sized pieces, so that they can be quickly pickled.

Put all the vegetables in a resealable plastic bag, then add the salt, kombu stock powder, golden caster sugar, yuzu zest (or orange and lime zest) and shichimi spice mix. Mix together inside the bag until all the vegetables are evenly coated in the seasonings.

Dip the bag in a bowl of cold water to remove any air and seal immediately so it is almost vacuum-packed.

Refrigerate and leave to pickle for at least 20 minutes and up to overnight.

Drain any water that has come out of the vegetables and then serve.

UMESU ZUKE
UME-FLAVOURED PICKLED RADISH

Presentation is key in Japanese cuisine and simple pickles can become works of art, adding a little poetry to your table. In this recipe, I want to share with you a special cutting technique used on pickled radishes. The cuts are in the shape of a grid, so when pickled, the radishes open up and look like chrysanthemum flowers! A pair of disposable chopsticks is my trick for holding the radishes steady while cutting them into the perfect shape.

6–8 red radishes, tops and bottoms
   trimmed off
3 tbsp umesu (salted plum seasoning)
3 tbsp mirin
1 tsp clear honey
a pinch of shichimi (Japanese spice mix),
   to serve (optional)

disposable chopsticks (not separated)

MAKES 6–8

Place the disposable chopsticks horizontally on a chopping board and put a radish between them with one of the trimmed ends facing up.

Make several small cuts widthways across the radish, cutting about two-thirds of the way down. Then rotate the radish 90 degrees and cut across the cuts you have already made, to create a tiny cross-hatch or grid shape. The chopsticks will help to hold the radish steady and make sure you don't cut right through. Repeat with all the radishes.

Mix together the umesu seasoning, mirin and honey in a bowl lined with clingfilm/plastic wrap. Add the radishes and close the plastic wrap to encase the radishes and seasonings.

Refrigerate and leave to pickle for 30 minutes – they will open up across the cuts! Squeeze excess seasonings out of the radishes. Sprinkle with shichimi to serve, if liked.

SHIRA AE
TOFU DIP WITH VEGETABLES

This is my grandma's tofu salad recipe, one of the most traditional 'aemono' or dressed salads. It literally means 'white mixture' because of the creamy texture of the mashed tofu. Even now, it is still a staple of Japanese home cooking.

300 g/10½ oz. silken tofu (soft tofu)
30 g/1 oz. konnyaku block (optional)
130 g/4¾ oz. mixture of watercress
    and spinach
2 tsp light soy sauce
2 tsp agave syrup
1 tbsp Japanese white sesame paste
    (or light tahini)
a pinch of salt
dried goji berries, soaked and
    drained, to garnish

SERVES 4 AS A SIDE

Wrap the tofu in plenty of paper towels and compress under a heavy kitchen utensil for 30 minutes to remove excess water.

Rub the konnyaku (if using) with a pinch of salt. Bring some water to the boil in a large saucepan and boil the konnyaku for 3 minutes to remove any smell, then drain and cut into 3-cm/1¼-inch length strips. Set aside.

Bring some water to the boil in another saucepan. Add the watercress and spinach and boil for 1 minute, then drain. Immediately rinse under cold water, then drain. Sprinkle with 1 teaspoon of the light soy sauce, then squeeze out water from the leaves. Use your hands to form the leaves into a cylinder shape and then chop into 3-cm/1¼-inch lengths. Set aside.

Combine the tofu, agave, sesame paste, remaining 1 teaspoon light soy sauce and salt in a food processor. Blend until smooth.

Mix the watercress and spinach and konnyaku with the tofu paste to combine well. Garnish with the goji berries and serve cold.

KABOCHA SALADA
PUMPKIN SALAD

Kabocha pumpkin is beautifully sweet, nutty and less watery than other varieties of pumpkin. Traditionally, we would serve kabocha simmered in soy dashi stock, but this is my modern take on a kabocha side dish. I particularly like the addition of raisins and almonds, it adds different textures and gives a beautiful autumnal feel to the dish.

400 g/14 oz. kabocha pumpkin
    (or delica pumpkin), deseeded
3 tbsp Japanese mayonnaise
1 tbsp natural/plain Greek-style yogurt
sea salt and freshly ground black pepper
20 g/¾ oz. raisins, to garnish
15 g/½ oz. flaked/slivered almonds,
    toasted, to garnish

SERVES 4 AS A SIDE

Dice the pumpkin into small pieces, leaving the skin on.

Place the pumpkin in a saucepan, cover with water and bring to the boil.

Turn down the heat, then simmer for 10 minutes until cooked through.

Drain, then leave to cool and dry for 20 minutes.

Mash half of the pumpkin using a potato masher or fork and mix together with the Japanese mayonnaise, yogurt and some salt and pepper to season.

Place the mashed pumpkin into a serving bowl and garnish with the remaining chunks of pumpkin, the raisins and the toasted flaked/slivered almonds. Serve cold.

3 DRESSED VEGETABLE SALADS

These aemono (dressed salads), are each simple to make and use few ingredients. The theme that ties them together is the roasted nutty taste of either white sesame, black sesame or pine nuts, which beautifully complements the vegetables.

WHITE SESAME DRESSING ON GREEN BEANS

200 g/7 oz. green beans
a pinch of salt
3 tbsp toasted white sesame seeds
1 tbsp soy sauce
1 tbsp mirin
½ tsp soft light brown sugar

SERVES 4 AS A SIDE

Boil the green beans in a saucepan of salted water for about 2 minutes. Do not overcook.

Drain the beans and rinse briefly under cold running water. Drain well again.

Trim the ends off the green beans diagonally, then cut them into 5 cm/2 inch lengths.

Use a suribachi (Japanese grinder) or a pestle and mortar to grind the toasted seeds to a paste. Place the paste in a bowl and then mix together with the soy sauce, mirin and sugar.

Dress the green beans with the sesame dressing just before serving cold.

BLACK SESAME SAUCE ON TENDERSTEM BROCCOLI

200 g/7 oz. tenderstem broccoli
a pinch of salt
3 tbsp toasted black sesame seeds
1 tbsp soy sauce
1 tbsp mirin
½ tsp soft light brown sugar

SERVES 4 AS A SIDE

Boil the broccoli in a saucepan of salted water for about 2 minutes. Do not overcook.

Drain the broccoli and rinse briefly under cold running water. Drain well again.

Trim the tenderstem broccoli, then cut diagonally into 5 cm/2 inch lengths. Set aside.

Use a suribachi (Japanese grinder) or a pestle and mortar to grind the toasted seeds to a paste. Place the paste in a small bowl and then mix together with the soy sauce, mirin and brown sugar.

Dress the broccoli with the sesame dressing just before serving cold.

PINE NUT DRESSING WITH CARROTS

3 tbsp toasted pine nuts
1 tbsp soy sauce
1 tbsp mirin
½ tsp soft light brown sugar
2 carrots, peeled and thinly
  sliced into strips

SERVES 4 AS A SIDE

Use a suribachi (Japanese grinder) or a pestle and mortar to grind the toasted pine nuts into a paste. Mix the paste with the soy sauce, mirin and sugar. Dress the carrots with the pine nut dressing just before serving.

WHITE SESAME DRESSING
ON GREEN BEANS

BLACK SESAME SAUCE ON
TENDERSTEM BROCCOLI

PINE NUT DRESSING
WITH CARROTS

AGE BITASHI
DEEP-FRIED MARINATED VEGETABLES

Age bitashi means 'fried and soaked' in Japanese. This is a lovely summery dish traditionally made with aubergine/eggplant and (bell) peppers.

500 ml/2 cups plus 2 tbsp vegetable oil
1 aubergine/eggplant, cut into 3-cm/
    1¼-inch x 7-cm/2¾-inch rectangular strips
1 red (bell) pepper, cut lengthways into strips
1 yellow (bell) pepper, cut lengthways into strips
6 okra
½ lemon

MARINADE
1 tsp umeboshi (pickled plum) paste
1 tsp peeled and grated fresh ginger
2 tbsp soy sauce
2 tbsp mirin
2 tbsp rice vinegar
200 ml/¾ cup Kombu & Katsuobushi
    (see page 24)

SERVES 4 AS A SIDE

In a small bowl, mix together the ginger and umeboshi paste, then add the soy sauce, mirin and vinegar and mix well. Stir in the dashi. Transfer the marinade to a small baking dish.

Heat the vegetable oil in a heavy-based saucepan to 180°C (350°F) over a high heat. Wipe off any water on the vegetables. Drop a piece of vegetable into the oil. If it gently sizzles, the oil is ready. Reduce the heat to medium to maintain the temperature.

Working in about five batches, deep-fry the vegetables for 2–3 minutes, turning twice. Remove and drain the excess oil. Cut the okra in half lengthways when cool enough to handle. Toss all the vegetables in the dish of marinade. Squeeze over the lemon and cover with clingfilm/plastic wrap. Let marinate for a minimum of 2 hours or overnight at room temperature. Serve cold.

YAKI BITASHI
FRIED & MARINATED VEGETABLES

Literally meaning 'fry and marinade', this is a great way of adding oomph to seasonal vegetables. The marinade is slightly sweet, salty and piquant, but you can still taste the fresh vegetables. This recipe is also good with padrón or shishito peppers, if you can find them in exotic grocery stores.

1 tbsp vegetable oil
100 g/3½ oz. tenderstem broccoli
100 g/3½ oz. asparagus, trimmed

MARINADE
1 tbsp soy sauce
1 tbsp mirin
1 tsp English mustard

SERVES 4 AS A SIDE

Add the vegetable oil to a ridged stove-top grill pan/griddle pan or frying pan/skillet over a medium heat. Add the broccoli and asparagus and fry for 2 minutes to brown the surface of vegetables and add some aromatic charred flavour. You want to keep the crunchy texture inside. Remove from the heat and place in a shallow heatproof dish.

For the marinade, stir together the soy sauce, mirin and English mustard in a bowl.

While the vegetables are still hot, pour over the marinade and mix gently. Leave the vegetables to cool and absorb the flavours.

Drain the seasonings, then cut the vegetables diagonally into 3-cm/1¼-inch lengths to serve (so that they are easier to eat with chopsticks). Serve cold.

4 DRESSINGS

Each of these four dressings will bring something unique to your dishes. Ume (made with umeboshi salted pickled plums) has a distinctly tangy, yet refreshing taste. Tart and citrusy yuzu ponzu is the classic Japanese all-purpose sauce. The 'Japanitalian' vinaigrette (inspired by my husband's native cuisine) is punchy yet well-balanced. Creamy goma miso is another classic Japanese dressing with a warm, nutty taste.

UME DRESSING

1 tbsp umeboshi (pickled plum) paste
2 tbsp vegetable oil
1 tbsp rice vinegar
1 tbsp mirin
1 tsp light soy sauce
1 tsp honey

small sterilized jar with a lid

MAKES ABOUT 75 ML/⅓ CUP

Combine all the ingredients together in the jar and mix well. Seal and refrigerate. The dressing will keep for up to 2 weeks.

YUZU PONZU DRESSING

110 ml/scant ½ cup light soy sauce
120 ml/½ cup yuzu juice
2 tbsp mirin
3 g/¹⁄₁₆ oz. katsuobushi (bonito flakes)
3-cm/1¼-inch piece of dried kombu

small sterilized jar with a lid

MAKES ABOUT 240 ML/1 CUP

Combine all the ingredients in the jar and mix well. Seal, refrigerate and leave to marinate for 1 week. Remove the katsuobushi and kombu before using. The dressing will keep for up to 2 weeks.

'JAPANITALIAN' DRESSING

150 ml/⅔ cup olive oil
75 ml/⅓ cup rice vinegar (or balsamic vinegar)
45 ml/3 tbsp soy sauce
2 tbsp clear honey
40 g/1½ oz. finely grated onion
40 g/1½ oz. finely grated carrot
4 finely chopped pitted black olives
sea salt and ground black pepper, to season

small sterilized jar with a lid

MAKES 350 ML/1½ CUPS

Combine all the ingredients in the jar, stir well to combine and seal. Refrigerate overnight so that the onion and carrot become mild and mature in the dressing. Stir well before serving. The dressing will keep for up to 2 weeks.

GOMA MISO DRESSING

90 ml/⅓ cup Japanese white sesame paste (or light tahini)
2 tbsp sweet white miso
120 ml/½ cup mirin
90 ml/⅓ cup light soy sauce
3 tbsp rice vinegar
1 tbsp freshly squeezed lemon juice
½ garlic clove, grated

small sterilized jar with a lid

MAKES ABOUT 350 ML/1½ CUPS

Whisk together the sesame paste and miso in a bowl, then slowly whisk in the mirin, then the soy sauce, then the vinegar. If you add these too quickly the paste may separate. Mix in the lemon juice and garlic. Place in the jar, seal and refrigerated. It will keep for up to 2 weeks.

'JAPANITALIAN'

GOMA MISO

YUZU PONZU

UME

DESSERTS

ANKO
SWEET AZUKI BEAN PASTE

Anko is an essential ingredient in wagashi and other Japanese confectioneries. It's simply made from azuki beans, water, sugar and a little salt. You might think it strange that we use beans as one of the main ingredients in our desserts, but azuki have a luscious, sweet nutty flavour to them and a texture that can be smooth or chunky. It's the sweet, slightly sticky element, a little bit like jam/jelly for us, so much so that we make 'an pan', bread filled with azuki bean paste. In shops, you can buy two different types of anko: koshian, the smooth version that has been finely mashed, and tsubuan, the grainy one which has been left untreated. This easy recipe is actually a cross between koshian and tsubuan, smooth but also grainy so it's easier to handle. The best of both worlds, really!

250 g/9 oz. dried azuki beans
200 g/1 cup golden caster
 sugar
a pinch of fine sea salt

MAKES 700 G/1 LB. 9 OZ.

Place the azuki beans in a sieve/strainer and rinse well under cold water. Transfer to a large saucepan and cover with twice the amount of water. Bring to the boil.

Once boiling, carefully drain the cooking water from the beans, and replace with twice the amount of fresh water. This will remove any bitter taste. Bring to the boil again, then turn the heat down to low and simmer, uncovered, for 45–60 minutes until soft. If the pan dries out, add some more water to keep the beans covered. When they start moving with the bubbles in the water, it means they are cooked. You can also remove a bean and squash it between your fingers to test if it's soft. Drain and reserve the cooking water.

Blend the beans to a smooth paste using a food processor or mash them well with a fork. Add some of the cooking water, if needed, to get a smooth texture. Put the paste back into the saucepan, mix in the sugar and simmer for 15 minutes over a low heat to thicken. Mix in the pinch of salt to season.

To help dry and cool the paste quickly, scoop up small portions with a spatula and spread out on a large plate or baking sheet. Leave the azuki bean paste to cool down completely, then store in a clean container (covered) in the refrigerator for up to 1 week. The paste will keep for up to 1 month in the freezer.

DORAYAKI
AZUKI BEAN PASTE PANCAKE SANDWICHES

If you're a novice in wagashi, this is the dessert for you. Japanese desserts can seem a bit daunting to start with. Dorayaki are comprised of the very Japanese sweet azuki bean paste Anko (see left), sandwiched between two American-inspired pancakes, so you're not completely out of your comfort zone taste-wise. If you're a fan of the robotic cat Doraemon, the hero of the eponymous anime cartoon, you would be aware of its unstoppable craving for dorayaki!

60 g/⅓ cup minus 1 tsp Anko
(Sweet Azuki Bean Paste),
see page opposite

PANCAKE BATTER
2 UK large/US extra-large
eggs
90 g/½ cup minus 1 tbsp
caster/granulated sugar
1 tbsp runny honey
1 tsp mirin
½ tsp bicarbonate of soda/
baking soda, sifted
100 g/¾ cup plain/
all-purpose flour, sifted

**AZUKI CREAM FILLING
VARIATION**
30 g/1 oz. Anko
(Sweet Azuki Bean Paste),
see page opposite
30 g/1 oz. crème fraîche
or mascarpone
1 tsp caster/granulated sugar

MAKES 4 SANDWICHES
(APPROX. 9-CM/3½-INCHES
IN DIAMETER)

For the pancake batter, break the eggs into a large mixing bowl. Add the sugar and whisk with the eggs until pale and fluffy.

Add the honey, mirin, sifted bicarbonate of soda/baking soda, flour and 2½ tablespoons of water. Mix together with a rubber spatula until all the ingredients are combined. Cover the bowl with clingfilm/plastic wrap, then rest in the refrigerator for 15 minutes. The mixture should be thick but dropping consistency when you pick up a spoonful.

Heat a large, non-stick frying pan/skillet over a medium heat and reduce the heat to low. Scoop up a large spoonful (a serving spoon or a heaped tablespoon) of pancake mixture and drop slowly into the pan, letting it fall into a round shape naturally. Don't add more batter or press the batter down.

Repeat to make 2–3 pancakes in the same pan. After 1–2 minutes, when a few bubbles appear on the surface, carefully turn the pancakes over using a thin spatula. Cook for about 3 minutes on the other side until golden, then transfer to a large tray to cool down. Repeat with the remaining batter to make eight pancakes.

To serve, sandwich some sweet azuki bean paste between two cooled pancakes and press gently together. Repeat to make three more sandwiches. Serve cold.

The dorayaki will keep for 2–3 days in a sealed box at room temperature.

VARIATION
For a creamier variation on the filling, mix the sweet azuki bean paste together with the crème fraîche or mascarpone and sugar. Use to sandwich the pancakes together. Keep these ones in the refrigerator for up to 2 days.

ICHIGO DAIFUKU
FRESH STRAWBERRY & AZUKI BEAN PASTE MOCHI

Not only is this one of the most popular Japanese confections inside and outside of Japan, but ichigo daifuku can also be your party's show-stopper! It consists of an outer layer of mochi with an azuki bean filling enclosing an entire fresh, juicy strawberry – making three delicious layers of contrasting colours and textures! The mochi-making part might sound a little complex, but it's actually as easy as making any dough. I also find the wrapping in mochi part particularly satisfying!

8 fresh strawberries
160 g/5¾ oz. Anko
   (Sweet Azuki Bean Paste),
   see page 172

MOCHI MIXTURE
100 g/3½ oz. shiratamako
   (glutinous short-grain
   mochi rice flour)
85 g/½ cup minus 1 tbsp
   caster/granulated sugar
katakuriko (potato starch)
   or cornflour/cornstarch,
   for dusting the work
   surface

steamer with a lid
muslin/cheesecloth

MAKES 8

Remove the hulls and trim the leaves from the top of the strawberries. Coat each strawberry in a layer of the sweet azuki bean paste, leaving the pointy bottom of each strawberry uncovered. Set aside.

Bring a steamer to the boil, lined with a piece of wet muslin/cheesecloth inside.

To make the mochi mixture, combine the shiratamako and sugar in a mixing bowl and slowly add 150 ml/⅔ cup cold water, mixing well to combine until smooth.

Pour the mochi mixture onto the wet muslin/cheesecloth in the hot steamer. Put the lid on and steam for 20 minutes. During the 20 minutes of steaming time, carefully remove the muslin/cheesecloth from the steamer, let the dough cool a little and then knead the dough in the muslin/cheesecloth. Do this about 3 times during the steaming process so that it cooks evenly.

After 20 minutes, when the mixture has become firm and translucent, remove the muslin for the last time and use damp hands to knead the mixture through while still fairly hot to make a smooth dough.

Sift some katakuriko (potato starch) or cornflour/cornstarch onto a clean work surface to provide a light dusting. Transfer the mochi mixture from the muslin/cheesecloth onto the work surface. Dust your hands in katakuriko to stop it from sticking and cut the mochi dough into eight even pieces.

Flatten each mochi with your palm into a round, thin disc, about 6.5 cm/2½ inches in diameter.

Wrap each azuki bean paste-covered strawberry carefully in a disc of the mochi dough, finishing by closing the open edges around the top of each strawberry. Press the open edges together and smooth down to seal the strawberry inside. Serve immediately. (These don't keep well and are best eaten on the day they are made.)

TOFU NO YAKI CHEESECAKE
BAKED TOFU CHEESECAKE

Adding tofu to this baked cheesecake recipe keeps it light and moist – each mouthful almost melts in the mouth. The touch of cinnamon and addition of lemon zest makes it the perfect dessert to comfort you when the colder days arrive. Perfect for eating while curled up in a cosy armchair with a hot cup of tea!

BASE
160 g/5¾ oz. digestive
   biscuits/graham crackers
60 g/½ stick butter, melted
1 tsp ground cinnamon

CHEESECAKE
350 g/12 oz. firm tofu
500 g/2¼ cups soft cheese
175 g/¾ cup plus 2 tbsp
   caster/granulated sugar
2 UK large/US extra-large
   eggs
finely grated zest of 1 lemon
seeds scraped from 1 vanilla
   pod/bean
200 g/7 oz. mixed fresh
   berries

*20-cm/8-inch round
   loose-based cake pan*

SERVES 6–8

For the cheesecake, wrap the tofu in plenty of paper towels and compress under a heavy kitchen utensil for 30 minutes to remove excess water.

Preheat the oven to 180°C (350°F) Gas 4.

For the cheesecake base, crush the biscuits/crackers to fine crumbs in a food processor or by putting them into a resealable bag and bashing them with a rolling pin. Transfer the crumbs to a mixing bowl and stir in the melted butter and cinnamon until well combined.

Spread the biscuit/cracker mixture evenly over the bottom of the cake pan and press down to flatten.

Combine the tofu and soft cheese in the rinsed out food processor, and blend to combine. Transfer to a bowl and add the sugar, eggs, lemon zest and vanilla seeds. Mix well until all the ingredients are evenly combined. Pour the mixture over the top of the biscuit/cracker base.

Bake in the preheated oven for 10 minutes, then reduce the oven temperature to 160°C (325°F) Gas 3 and bake for a further 45–50 minutes.

Turn the oven off and allow the cheesecake to cool completely for 2–3 hours in the oven, which should help stop cracks from forming.

Remove from the oven and leave at room temperature for a few hours before transferring to the refrigerator and chilling overnight.

The next day, remove the cheesecake from its pan, transfer to a serving plate and scatter fresh berries on top to serve.

MITARASHI DANGO
MOCHI BALLS ON SKEWERS

Mitarashi dango is a very traditional wagashi dessert of skewered balls of mochi. The mochi are then slathered in mitarashi, a slightly sticky sweet and salty sauce. The making process might seem deceptively laborious at first but it's actually very easy to do and not too time consuming. Give it a go and enjoy trying something new!

120 g/4¼ oz. joshinko
   (short-grain rice flour)
100 g/3½ oz. shiratamako
   (glutinous short-grain
   mochi rice flour)
20 g/1½ tbsp caster/
   granulated sugar
175 ml/¾ cup warm water
   (about 50°C/122°F)
oil, for the work surface

MITARASHI SAUCE
2 tbsp soy sauce
1 tsp mirin
3 tbsp brown sugar
1 tbsp katakuriko (potato
   starch) or cornflour/
   cornstarch mixed with
   1 tbsp cold water

steamer with a lid
muslin/cheesecloth
10 wooden skewers
   (10-cm/4-inch length),
   soaked in water
cook's blowtorch (optional)

MAKES 10 SKEWERS

Bring a steamer to the boil, lined with a piece of wet muslin/cheesecloth inside.

In a large mixing bowl, combine the joshinko, shiratamako and sugar using a spatula. Slowly add the warm water and mix to a dough. The texture should be as smooth as an earlobe. Divide the dough into four pieces.

Put the mochi mixture onto the wet muslin/cheesecloth in the hot steamer. Put the lid on and steam for 30 minutes. During the 30 minutes of steaming time, carefully remove the muslin/cheesecloth from the steamer, let the dough cool a little and then knead the dough in the muslin/cheesecloth. Do this about 3 times during the steaming process so that it cooks evenly.

After 30 minutes, when the mixture has become firm and translucent, remove the muslin for the last time and use damp hands to knead the mixture through while still fairly hot to make a smooth dough. If it sticks, lightly oil the work surface. Form the dough into a long cylinder, then cut into 30 even pieces. Shape each piece into a ball, roughly the size of a cherry tomato.

Thread three balls onto each skewer. Blowtorch the surface of skewered dangos or place under a hot grill/broiler for 1–2 minutes, this creates a wonderful scorched aroma and a crunchy texture on the outside.

To make the mitarashi sauce, combine the soy sauce, mirin and brown sugar with 60 ml/¼ cup water in a small saucepan and bring to the boil. Reduce the heat to low and slowly stir in the katakuriko (potato starch) or cornflour/cornstarch mixture. Simmer for 1–2 minutes, stirring, until thickened.

Place the mochi skewers on serving plates and drizzle with the mitarashi sauce to serve.

If you have any mochi leftover, they will harden up overnight, but just warm them through in a steamer and they will soften again.

MATCHA NO TIRAMISU
GREEN TEA TIRAMISU

My husband being Italian, I quickly learnt from his mother how to make the perfect tiramisu. I love this dessert, and who doesn't?! One morning, I thought I'd tweak it a little bit to give it a Japanese touch. The tofu is a great addition to the mascarpone and holds beautifully. The matcha lends its beautiful vibrant green colour and earthy taste to the sweet cake. Almost too beautiful to eat but impossible to resist!

150 g/5½ oz. firm tofu

3 UK large/US extra-large eggs

75 g/⅓ cup plus 2 tsp golden caster sugar

350 g/1½ cups mascarpone

a pinch of fine sea salt

½ tbsp matcha powder, plus extra to decorate

150 ml/⅔ cup hot water

50 ml/3½ tbsp rum (optional)

175 g/6 oz. sponge fingers

1.5-litre/quart glass serving dish

SERVES 6

Wrap the tofu in plenty of paper towels and compress under a heavy kitchen utensil for 30 minutes to remove excess water.

When drained, place in a food processor and blend to a smooth paste. Set aside.

Separate the egg yolks and whites into two large mixing bowls. Use a hand-held electric whisk to beat the egg yolks with half of the sugar until creamy and the sugar has dissolved. Set aside.

Beat together the mascarpone and blended tofu together in a third mixing bowl to a paste.

Gradually add the egg yolk mixture to the mascarpone mixture in batches, whisking in until smooth. Set aside.

Whisk the egg whites to soft peaks, then add the salt and the rest of the sugar and whisk to stiff peaks.

Gradually fold the egg white mixture into the egg yolk and mascarpone mixture. Set aside.

Put the matcha into a small mixing bowl and pour over a couple of spoonfuls of the hot water. Whisk together to dissolve any lumps, then add the rest of the hot water and stir. Add the rum (if using) and leave to cool.

Dip the sponge fingers into the matcha tea, one at a time, until soaked but not too softened, and arrange in a single layer over the bottom of the glass dish.

Spread half of the mascarpone mixture over the sponge fingers and smooth over the surface.

Repeat the process for the second layer, soaking the remaining sponge fingers and placing them on top of the mascarpone. Spread the second layer of mascarpone mixture over the top and smooth over.

Refrigerate for at least 2 hours or ideally overnight before eating.

Just before serving, dust the top of the tiramisu with some extra matcha powder to decorate.

YUZU TO TOFU NO RARE CHEESECAKE

YUZU & TOFU NO-BAKE CHEESECAKES

These no-bake cheesecakes are super creamy and almost velvety thanks to the combination of both soft cheese and silken tofu. Refreshing and fragrant yuzu is a small Japanese citrus fruit used in so many dishes, both savoury and sweet. You can now find yuzu juice in big supermarkets in the Asian section, but if you can't find yuzu jam/jelly, marmalade works just as well. I like to make this dessert in separate individual glasses or jars for a beautiful kawaii presentation!

BASE
90 g/3¼ oz. digestive
   biscuits/graham crackers
30 g/2 tbsp butter, melted

CHEESECAKE
2 gelatine leaves
40 ml/2¾ tbsp yuzu juice
175 g/6 oz. silken tofu
   (soft tofu)
150 g/⅔ cup cream cheese
100 ml/scant ½ cup double/
   heavy cream
50 g/¼ cup caster/granulated
   sugar
30 g/1 oz. yuzu jam/jelly
   (or orange marmalade),
   plus extra to serve
seeds scraped from ½ vanilla
   pod/bean

*5 serving glasses or glass jars
   (approx. 180 ml/¾ cup)*

MAKES 5

For the cheesecake bases, crush the biscuits/crackers to fine crumbs in a food processor or by putting them into a resealable bag and bashing them with a rolling pin. Transfer the crumbs to a mixing bowl and stir in the melted butter until well combined.

Divide the biscuit/cracker mixture evenly between the five glasses or jars and press down firmly to flatten.

To make the cheesecake, soak the gelatine leaves in a bowl of cold water for 3 minutes to soften.

Squeeze the excess water out and transfer the gelatine to a small saucepan. Add the yuzu juice and stir together over a low heat until just melted and combined. Be careful not to let the gelatine boil. Set aside to cool.

Combine the tofu, soft cheese, double/heavy cream, sugar, yuzu jam/jelly (or orange marmalade), vanilla seeds and cooled yuzu gelatine in a food processor and blend until smooth. Alternatively, you can simply mash the tofu until smooth, then whisk in the rest of the ingredients by hand in a bowl until smooth and thick.

Spoon the cheesecake mixture into the glasses or jars over the biscuit/cracker bases. Remove any air from the containers by tapping them lightly on the work surface. Refrigerate for 2 hours to set.

Top with extra yuzu jam/jelly or marmalade to serve. The cheesecakes will keep for 5 days refrigerated.

ALMOND KUZU TOFU
GELATINE-& DAIRY-FREE PANNA COTTA WITH BLUEBERRY SAUCE

Panna cotta is always popular, and this dairy-and gelatine-free recipe will delight anyone with its incredibly creamy texture. I use kuzu as a setting agent, which is a plant-based starch used in many Japanese dishes. Kuzu is a raw ingredient that needs to be cooked – the longer the cooking time, the firmer the texture becomes. You can use any other type of non-dairy milk if you prefer, but I find that almond milk gives a lovely nutty taste. This looks so decadent, especially served with the berry sauce, but it's actually very easy to make!

50 g/1¾ oz. kuzu
500 ml/2 cups plus 2 tbsp unsweetened almond milk
90 ml/⅓ cup agave syrup
seeds scraped from ⅓ vanilla pod/bean
a pinch of salt

BLUEBERRY SAUCE
100 g/3½ oz. blueberries
1 tsp freshly squeezed lemon juice
2 tbsp agave syrup

approx. 15 x 10-cm/4 x 6-inch rectangular plastic container, about 5 cm/ 2 inches deep

SERVES 6

Combine the kuzu, almond milk, agave syrup, vanilla seeds and salt in a saucepan. Place over a medium heat and stir constantly until the kuzu has dissolved.

Reduce the heat to low and keep stirring constantly for 7–10 minutes. The more you cook, the thicker the texture will get. When the mixture has thickened to the texture of a custard, turn the heat off.

Wet a rectangular plastic container with a bit of water and then pour the mixture in – the water helps to stop the panna cotta from sticking to the surface of the container.

Cover with wet clingfilm/plastic wrap and leave to cool. Once cool, refrigerate for at least 1 hour. It should be solid enough for you to cut into portions.

Meanwhile, to make the blueberry sauce, combine the blueberries, lemon juice and agave syrup in a saucepan. Cook over a low heat for 3–5 minutes until the blueberries have mostly broken down. Leave to cool, then refrigerate.

When the panna cotta is set, remove the clingfilm/ plastic wrap and place a chopping board on top of the container. Flip the container and chopping board together to drop the panna cotta onto the chopping board.

Wet a knife and cut the panna cotta into 6 squares.

Serve in individual bowls drizzled with the chilled blueberry sauce.

GOMA SENBEI
SESAME SNAPS WITH MISO CARAMEL SAUCE

If you have a sweet tooth, you will agree that caramel goes so well with a touch of salt. You may have already tried 'caramel au beurre salé' (caramel with salted butter) and found it hard to put your spoon down. This recipe is the Japanese version of that, in which I use miso instead of salted butter – you get your salty hit but also a greater depth of umami flavour. You might also remind yourself that miso is full of probiotics which aid digestion, so you'd better have another spoonful!

40 g/3¼ tbsp golden caster sugar
2 tbsp butter
2 tbsp runny honey
1 tbsp yuzu juice (or other citrus juice)
25 g/3 tbsp plain/all-purpose flour
25 g/2¼ tbsp toasted white sesame
20 g/2 tbsp toasted black sesame seeds
finely grated zest of ½ orange
vanilla ice cream, to serve

MISO CARAMEL SAUCE
150 g/¾ cup caster/granulated sugar
50 ml/3½ tbsp water
100 ml/scant ½ cup crème fraîche (or double/heavy cream)
30 g/1 oz. white miso

baking sheet, lined with baking parchment

SERVES 6

Preheat the oven to 180°C (350°F) Gas 4.

Bring the sugar, butter and honey to the boil in a small saucepan until melted together, then add the yuzu or other citrus juice.

Remove from the heat and stir in the flour and toasted white and black sesame seeds and orange zest. Leave until the mixture is cool enough to handle and the texture of soft toffee.

Form into 12 small balls and space out 4–5 balls on the lined baking sheet (they will melt down and spread out quite a bit). Bake in the preheated oven for 6–7 minutes until only just lightly browned. Leave to cool completely before carefully removing from the baking parchment.

Repeat for the remaining balls of dough.

The sesame snaps will keep in an airtight container for up to 1 week.

To make the miso caramel sauce, in a small saucepan, stir together the sugar and water to combine.

Put over a medium-high heat and cook, without stirring, for about 7 minutes until the sugar has turned into a golden-coloured caramel.

When the caramel is ready, remove from the heat and slowly whisk in the crème fraîche or cream. Some lumps will appear because of the temperature difference, but gently whisk to break them up and get a smooth texture. Finally, whisk in the miso until smooth. Serve the miso caramel sauce slightly warm on top of scoops of vanilla ice cream, with sesame snaps on the side.

INDEX

ACKNOWLEDGEMENTS

I left my hometown long ago now, and I would never have imagined that 15 years on, I would be writing my second cookbook on Japanese cuisine and celebrating over 10 years of Atsuko's Kitchen cookery classes in London.

This book would not exist without the enormous support and dedication from you all: I miei amori, my three boys: my husband Michele Rossi, our son Nicolo and his soon-to-be little brother (I am pregnant while working on this book). I couldn't dream of a more supportive and loving family. My life has never been so exciting and beautiful since you all came into it. Thank you for allowing me to do what I am so passionate about. I have so much love and gratitude for my parents in Japan (Yuriko and Hideki Ikeda): they taught me about my roots, made me appreciate Japan's incredible culture and history and most of all, instilled respect into me for this inherited tradition. Grazie mille to my parents in Italy for being so inspiring and for providing such wonderful support for my family.

A million thanks to my publisher, Cindy Richards for believing in me by giving me the opportunity to publish a second cookbook. An enormous thank you also to the hard working team at RPS: Leslie Harrington, Megan Smith, Alice Sambrook and Julia Charles, thank you for taking such good care of me and for making this book meaningful and graceful.

Thank you to my creative team: photographer Yuki Sugiura, what a pleasure to work with you again on my second cookbook. You have captured my cuisine beautifully with your Japanese aesthetic. Alexander Breeze, for selecting delicate and beautiful props for my dishes. Risa Sano (Mentsen) for providing illustrations with such an eclectic, stylish and modern touch. My efficient and reliable assistants, Masako, Michiyo and Mari for your dedication to both my classes and this book.

This book has also had wonderful contributions from my dear friends: Elsa Gleeson, your explanations of Japanese cuisine made all the introductions to the dishes in this book understandable and relatable for Western eyes. Beyond that, I am grateful for your endless support. Natsuki Kikuya (Museum of Sake), the Sake Samurai, thank you for your knowledgeable introduction to sake and the selection of sake tools, they have given depth to this book. Special thanks to Sansho for your contribution of beautiful Japanese ceramics for the photo shoot.

My gratitude extends even further, to all my friends for their encouragement and advice, and to my student friends who first came to my newly opened classes at Atsuko's Kitchen back in 2008. You have encouraged me and given purpose to my teaching career.

A huge thank you to every single student who has ever attended my classes, and an extra thank you to those who keep returning to my classes over the years.

All of you have made Atsuko's Kitchen what it is!